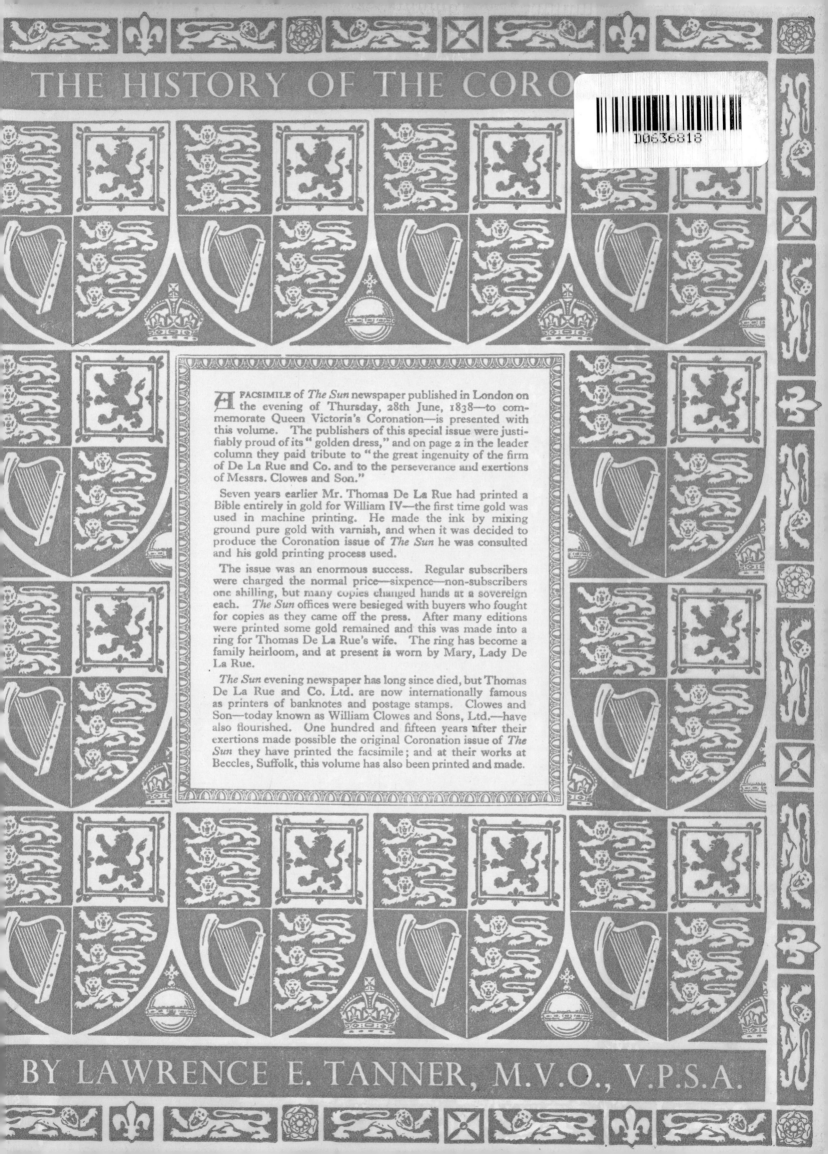

THE HISTORY OF THE CORO[NATION]

A FACSIMILE of *The Sun* newspaper published in London on the evening of Thursday, 28th June, 1838—to commemorate Queen Victoria's Coronation—is presented with this volume. The publishers of this special issue were justifiably proud of its " golden dress," and on page 2 in the leader column they paid tribute to "the great ingenuity of the firm of De La Rue and Co. and to the perseverance and exertions of Messrs. Clowes and Son."

Seven years earlier Mr. Thomas De La Rue had printed a Bible entirely in gold for William IV—the first time gold was used in machine printing. He made the ink by mixing ground pure gold with varnish, and when it was decided to produce the Coronation issue of *The Sun* he was consulted and his gold printing process used.

The issue was an enormous success. Regular subscribers were charged the normal price—sixpence—non-subscribers one shilling, but many copies changed hands at a sovereign each. *The Sun* offices were besieged with buyers who fought for copies as they came off the press. After many editions were printed some gold remained and this was made into a ring for Thomas De La Rue's wife. The ring has become a family heirloom, and at present is worn by Mary, Lady De La Rue.

The Sun evening newspaper has long since died, but Thomas De La Rue and Co. Ltd. are now internationally famous as printers of banknotes and postage stamps. Clowes and Son—today known as William Clowes and Sons, Ltd.—have also flourished. One hundred and fifteen years after their exertions made possible the original Coronation issue of *The Sun* they have printed the facsimile; and at their works at Beccles, Suffolk, this volume has also been printed and made.

BY LAWRENCE E. TANNER, M.V.O., V.P.S.A.

THE HISTORY OF THE
CORONATION

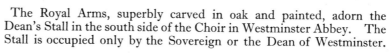

The Royal Arms, superbly carved in oak and painted, adorn the
Dean's Stall in the south side of the Choir in Westminster Abbey. The
Stall is occupied only by the Sovereign or the Dean of Westminster.

First Published December 1952
Reprinted December 1952
Reprinted January 1953
PRINTED IN GREAT BRITAIN AT BECCLES, SUFFOLK, BY WILLIAM CLOWES & SONS, LTD
FOR THE PUBLISHERS, BRITISH BOOK CENTRE, INC., 122 EAST 55th STREET, NEW YORK 22, N.Y.
IN ASSOCIATION WITH PITKIN PICTORIALS LTD., LONDON, W.C.1.

Elizabeth the Second, by the Grace of God of the United Kingdom of Great Britain and Northern Ireland and of her other Realms and Territories Queen, Head of the Commonwealth, Defender of the Faith. Her Majesty succeeded to the Throne on 6th February, 1952, on the death of her father, King George VI, and will be crowned in Westminster Abbey on 2nd June, 1953, the thirty-eighth Coronation to be celebrated at Westminster since 1066. The Queen was born in Bruton Street, London, on 21st April, 1926, and on the 20th November, 1947, she was married in Westminster Abbey to His Royal Highness the Duke of Edinburgh, K.G.

The style of the Queen's title reproduced above is applicable to the United Kingdom, the Colonies and Protectorates only. For each of the Commonwealth countries a separate title was proposed at the Common-wealth Prime Ministers' Conference in December, 1952. In the cases of Canada, Australia and New Zealand, the title is the same as for the United Kingdom except that the name of each country replaces the words "of Great Britain and Northern Ireland." In South Africa, the Queen's title is: Elizabeth the Second, Queen of South Africa and of her other Realms and Terri-tories, Head of the Commonwealth. In Pakistan Her Majesty's title is: Elizabeth the Second, Queen of the United Kingdom and of her other Realms and Terri-tories, Head of the Commonwealth, and for Ceylon, the form of title is the same as for South Africa except, of course, that "Ceylon" replaces "South Africa." For India, no formal title is used, but the Republic recognises the Queen as "Head of the Commonwealth," and these words appear in all the other titles.

The officers of the College of Arms assembled at St. James's Palace on the occasion of the reading of the Coronation Proclamation of Queen Elizabeth II. They are appointed by the Sovereign by Letters Patent under the Great Seal on the nomination of the Duke of Norfolk, Earl Marshal of England, who is responsible for the Ceremonies of State. On page 45 the duties of the Earl Marshal and the Foundation of the College are described.

The officers of the College of Arms (*from left to right*): Blue-mantle, Mr. J. A. Frere; Windsor Herald, Mr. R. P. Graham-Vivian; Richmond Herald, Mr. A. R. Wagner; York Herald, Mr. A. J. Toppin; Clarenceux King of Arms, Sir Arthur S. Cochrane; Garter King of Arms, the Hon. Sir George Bellew; The Earl Marshal of England, the Duke of Norfolk; Portcullis, the Master of Sinclair; Norroy and Ulster King of Arms, Sir Gerald Wollaston; Rouge Dragon, Mr. R. Mirrlees; Lancaster Herald, Mr. A. G. B. Russell; Chester Herald, Mr. J. D. Heaton-Armstrong; Rouge Croix, Mr. J. R. Bromhead Walker; and Somerset Herald, Major M. R. Trappes-Lomax.

THE HISTORY OF THE
CORONATION

by

LAWRENCE E. TANNER, M.V.O., V.P.S.A.

Keeper of the Muniments and Library, Westminster Abbey

PITKIN · LONDON

The Collegiate Church of St. Peter in Westminster is the full but unfamiliar title of the church known the breadth of the world more simply as "The Abbey." Three houses of worship have been raised on the site. Of the first little is known; of the second —King Edward the Confessor's creation—only a glorious heritage remains, but the third, built by Henry III, stands today, the unifying link between Church and State and People, and the bond by which, for 700 years, each Sovereign has been bound to the next. Here is seen the western end of the Abbey dominated by the twin towers completed from designs by Hawksmoor in 1745.

4

CONTENTS

With one hundred and eleven half-tone illustrations.

Henry III intended that his Abbey Church should be the crowning place of his successors. With this purpose in view he departed from traditional practice by placing the Choir and Choir Stalls west of the central crossing thus leaving a deep space between the Choir and the steps leading up to the Sanctuary and High Altar. It is in this central space—technically termed the "Theatre"—on a platform raised to the level of the Sanctuary that the greater part of the Coronation Ceremony takes place. This photograph, taken from the Choir Stalls, includes almost all the Theatre. The Coronation Chair is placed midway between the two great pillars above what normally would be the Altar steps. In the foreground on five raised steps is the Sovereign's Throne, and, since the arrangement of the Theatre seen here was for the Coronation of King George VI and Queen Elizabeth, the Consort's Throne is beside but two steps lower. Three chairs for the Royal Princes stand in the South Transept before the tiers of seats for the peers (right of the photograph), and beyond on the same side between the pillars is the Royal Gallery. In front of the Royal Gallery are the Chairs of State and faldstools used by the King and Queen at the beginning of the Ceremony.

THE CORONATION SETTING

WESTMINSTER ABBEY is so inseparably connected with the Coronation that it is easy to forget that Coronations in themselves are only one of the more conspicuous threads by which the Abbey is entwined with the history of the nation. Indeed, in one sense, those great national events make little impression on the Abbey itself. For a few brief months its interior is transformed. A broad and carpeted procession-way, flanked by galleries, leads from the West Door to the Choir. In the central space between the Transepts stand the Throne and the historic Coronation Chair. From the floor to the great Rose Windows and the Clerestory rise tier upon tier of seats filling, on the day, the space between the pointed arches and the grey stone walls with almost unimaginable colour. All this makes a superb and splendid setting for a great and solemn Service of dedication and consecration. But a Coronation passes. In a few more months the Abbey once again becomes a place of prayer and pilgrimage. Only the Coronation Chair remains to bear witness that one more memory has been added to the age-long history of the Abbey church.

Something, therefore, may be said here of that history and how it has come about that the Abbey has become the central shrine of the English-speaking peoples. By setting the Coronation in this perspective it may, perhaps, help us to realise its true significance and meaning.

The greater part of the present Westminster Abbey was built under the direction of King Henry III in the middle of the 13th century. It was the third church to stand upon the site. No trace has ever been found of the earliest of these churches, but we know that at some unknown date, long before the Norman Conquest, a little band of monks came and settled on what was then an island in the Thames—the Isle of Thorns as it was called, or Thorney Isle—and built a small church there. It is believed to have stood a little to the west of the present church. In later days the monks believed that it had been miraculously consecrated by St. Peter himself, and that it was in consequence under his special protection.

It was this fact which induced Edward the Confessor to choose Westminster as a place of residence, and to replace the primitive little Saxon church by a nobler church which came to be so indivisibly linked with his name. The building of this church became the absorbing interest of the King's later years. It was ready for consecration in December 1065, but he himself was too ill to attend the Ceremony. A few days later he was laid to rest within its walls. This great church, too, was to share the fate of its predecessor, but some of the monastic buildings remain, and excavations have shown that the ground plan of the church itself was not very much shorter than that of the existing church. It was, in fact, the largest church hitherto constructed either in England or in Normandy.

For a hundred and fifty years or so it remained untouched, and it was to witness the Coronations of William the Conqueror and his successors. Then, in 1245, King Henry III decided to pull it down and to build the present church. He was moved to do so partly by his own great veneration for the memory of Edward the Confessor and by his desire to provide a worthy setting for a new Shrine to contain the bones of the Saint, and, perhaps, even more by his admiration for the great French cathedrals—Rheims, Amiens, and Chartres—which were then newly built or building. Henry was himself a great patron of the arts, and at Westminster he employed the finest craftsmen of the time. The architect was Henry of Reyns, who was almost certainly an Englishman. But both he and his successors, John of Gloucester and Robert of Beverley, had studied the new French cathedrals. They did not hesitate to adopt what they thought good, but the building which they evolved at Westminster has not only been described as "triumphantly English" but is of a beauty which has never ceased to fascinate those upon whom it has laid its spell.

It must always be remembered that Westminster is an Abbey church, that is to say it was built primarily for the use of some eighty monks, and not for a modern congregation. Normally, in medieval times, the general public were not admitted to the church except as pilgrims, when they followed a definite route. There was, however, one exception when space had to be found for those who attended a great ceremony. By the 13th century Westminster had definitely become the Coronation church. Henry of Reyns, therefore, deliberately adopted a feature of the Confessor's church and placed his Choir west of the central crossing. This enabled the central space, between the Choir and the Sanctuary and High Altar, to be used in medieval times, as it is today, as the place where Coronations could take place.

By 1269 the East End with the Shrine, the Transepts, and the Choir had been completed, but the Confessor's Nave was allowed to remain. It continued to stand, linked on to the new work, until a hundred years later. Then, in 1375, it was decided to rebuild it under the direction of the great medieval architect, Henry Yevele. He designed the new Nave to copy the earlier 13th-century work. The result is that the whole Abbey appears today, at first sight, to have been built at the same time. Actually, for one reason or another, the work on the Nave was delayed, and it was only finally completed at the beginning of the 16th century. Meanwhile, and whilst the Nave was still unfinished, King Henry VII started to

ST. EDWARD'S CHAPEL

The Shrine of The Confessor in St. Edward's Chapel behind the High Altar was erected by Henry III, and was the chief glory of his new Abbey Church. It was completed in 1269 and around it were later placed the tombs of eight medieval Kings and Queens. For several centuries the Chapel was the centre of pilgrimage.

The Shrine is of Italian workmanship with a Purbeck marble base which was originally covered with glass mosaic and richly adorned with beautiful cameos and golden statues. The body of the Saint is buried above the niches in the sides of the Shrine, and the original gold Feretery was replaced in the reign of Queen Mary Tudor by the wooden structure which is seen in the photograph above. At the west end of the Shrine is an Altar which is used during the Coronation Service, and on this are now placed the candlesticks of wrought silver which were presented by King George VI and Queen Elizabeth on the occasion of their marriage.

In this Chapel is erected the Traverse (*left*), a small compartment shut off by a curtain to which the Sovereign retires in order to change the Royal robes during the course of the Coronation Service and at the Recess. It is in the Traverse that the Sovereign is vested with the purple velvet robes trimmed with ermine which are worn on leaving the church.

replace the original 13th-century Lady Chapel by the beautiful Chapel which bears his name. It was completed in 1519. Henceforth, except for the addition of the Western Towers in 1734-45, there was no further building at Westminster.

In 1540 the Monastery at Westminster was dissolved. Throughout medieval times successive Kings had taken a deep interest in its welfare. They had enriched the fabric of the church with gifts, and they had endowed the Monastery with lands. They had lived in the Palace nearby, and the Abbey had been not merely the place of their Coronation but the place where they were laid to rest. The departure of the monks meant a period of doubt and uncertainty. But a new chapter was to open with the foundation by Queen Elizabeth I, in 1560, of "the Collegiate Church of St. Peter in Westminster." A dean and prebendaries with a collegiate establishment took the place of the abbot and monks, and the little school within the precincts, founded and fostered by the monks, became and remained a part of the new foundation. In the following centuries it was to contribute many who have held high positions in Church and State.

Above all, and this was a fact of outstanding importance, the church which had hitherto been used only by the monks became a church to which all could resort, and gathered to itself new traditions and new inspirations. Thereby it tended to play an increasing part in the life of the nation as a whole. The process was a gradual one and it took many forms. Perhaps the most conspicuous feature was the increasing desire to be buried in Westminster Abbey. This was no longer the prerogative of Kings and their favourites. They, indeed, continued to be buried in Henry VII's Chapel, but, in addition, more and more monuments and tablets began to crowd the walls of the Abbey itself. The poets and writers tended to gather round Chaucer and Spenser in the South Transept, the statesmen round Chatham in the North Transept, the musicians round Purcell in the Choir Aisle, the men of science round Newton by the entry to the Choir, and the soldiers and sailors in the Nave. As the available space decreased, and as, too, the Abbey came to have a wider significance, it came to be felt that burial within its walls was an honour to be reserved only for the pre-eminently great.

But Westminster Abbey is neither a mausoleum nor a museum. It is, and has been for over a thousand years, primarily a church. It has been called, indeed, "the parish church of the English-speaking peoples," and as Dean Don, the present dean, has truly said "belonging to no diocese, it belongs to all." And so it is to its services, both every day and on great occasions, that we turn when we seek to find one of the main threads which have entwined it with the history of the nation; and of these services the Coronation is the most conspicuous and the most historic.

THE HIGH ALTAR

The High Altar is seen above as vested for the Coronation of King George VI and Queen Elizabeth. The Frontal of Cloth of Gold enriched with embroidery and bearing their Coat-of-Arms was presented for the Coronation by the King and Queen. Before the High Altar are the two faldstools used by Their Majesties during the Communion Service and facing it is the historic Coronation Chair dating from 1300.

Above the High Altar is a modern mosaic depicting "The Last Supper," and behind is the superb carved stone Screen erected during the reign of Henry VI. Through the archways in this Screen the Sovereign passes to the Traverse in St. Edward's Chapel.

To the south of the High Altar is the Royal Gallery (*left*) immediately above the tomb of Queen Anne of Cleves. It occupies the site of the medieval Royal pew. In front of the Gallery are the Chairs of State occupied by the Sovereign and his Consort at the beginning of the Coronation Service.

Henry IV, a reproduction of whose effigy in Canterbury Cathedral is seen above, contributed to Coronation history by founding the Order of the Bath before his crowning in 1399, and to the history of Westminster Abbey by dying in the Jerusalem Chamber in 1413 after being taken ill during a service. Legend relates that the King's death was engineered by the witchcraft of his Queen.

THE ABBEY OF KINGS

On this page some of the Kings of England most closely associated with Westminster are portrayed. The likeness of Henry VII and the effigies of Henry III and Henry IV are contemporary; the others are later and possibly inaccurate representations. TOP LEFT: Edward, called the Confessor, the founder. He was crowned at Winchester, 1043, and two years later married Eadgyth (Edith) daughter of Earl Godwine of Wessex. Edward built the Abbey as the price of the Pope's absolution for breaking his vow to make a pilgrimage to Rome. He was buried before the High Altar of his newly completed church 1066. TOP CENTRE: Henry III, crowned first at Gloucester 1216 and again at Westminster 1220 by direction of the Pope. He commenced the present fabric 1245, and in 1268 moved the Confessor's remains to a magnificent shrine, which is still the wonder of the Abbey. ABOVE CENTRE: Henry VII. The Crown was first placed upon his head on Bosworth Field as a symbol of victory after his defeat of Richard III 1485. He celebrated his Coronation in the Abbey the same year, and in 1503 he laid the foundations of the chapel of extraordinary beauty which bears his name. Henry VII died in 1509 and rests with his Queen, Elizabeth of York, in his chapel. RIGHT: William the Conqueror, whose veneration for the Confessor was such that he chose to be crowned in his Abbey Church—the first Coronation undoubtedly to be celebrated there.

For recent Coronations a temporary structure, known as the Annexe, has been built on to the western end of the Abbey. No part of the Ceremony takes place there, its purpose is to facilitate the forming of the complicated Procession before it passes through the West Door into the Nave, and to provide robing and retiring rooms for the Sovereign, the Royal Family, and the peerage. In the photograph above the exterior of the Annexe built for King George VI's Coronation is shown. The State Coach has just drawn up at the entrance and Their Majesties are alighting. Below is a view of the interior of the Annexe and the West Door.

THE LIBER REGALIS

The illustration above is taken from the *Liber Regalis* now in the Library of Westminster Abbey. This 14th-century MS. Order of Service was probably used by the Sovereigns themselves at their Coronations from Henry IV to Elizabeth I. It is likely that the MS. was actually written and illuminated for the Coronation of Queen Anne of Bohemia, the wife of King Richard II, in 1382, for it shows Germanic influence.

The King is in a blue robe and is depicted seated crowned in his Coronation Chair with (probably) the Archbishop of Canterbury and the Abbot of Westminster on either side of him. Behind stand two nobles. This photograph is reproduced by kind permission of the Dean and Chapter of Westminster.

The lower illustration shows the King's Stone still preserved at Kingston-on-Thames, Surrey, upon which seven Saxon Kings are said to have been enthroned. It was last used in 998, after which Kings chose to be crowned elsewhere, until William the Conqueror decided upon Westminster as the place for his Coronation in 1066 and this precedent has been followed ever since.

2

ORIGINS OF THE SERVICE

HEN Queen Elizabeth II is crowned in Westminster Abbey it will be the thirty-eighth Coronation of a reigning Sovereign to have taken place at Westminster since the Norman Conquest, and the twenty-eighth to have taken place within the existing Abbey church. In addition to these, however, Prince Henry, the eldest son of King Henry II, was crowned at Westminster during his father's lifetime, although he did not live to succeed to the Throne, and eleven Queen Consorts have been crowned some years after their husbands within the Abbey.

Coronations, therefore, have been associated with Westminster for nine hundred years. They are the most continuous succession of events that the Abbey has witnessed. As Dean Stanley pointed out, "none such belongs to any other building in the world. The Coronations of the Kings of France at Reims, and of the Popes in the Basilica of the Vatican, most nearly approach it. But Reims is now deserted, and the present Church of St. Peter is by five centuries more modern than the Abbey." And yet there are other places in England which preserve an even earlier tradition. The first Christian consecration of an Anglo-Saxon King of which we have any record took place in 785, perhaps at Chelsea, when Offa, King of Mercia, had his son, Egfrith, anointed and crowned as his successor. It was probably the first occasion on which the Frankish custom of anointing was practised in England, and it may well be that from that date it became a permanent feature of the inauguration of a King in this country.

In the 10th century the place usually chosen for Coronations, although for no very apparent reason, was Kingston-on-Thames. There, on the "King's stone," which is still carefully preserved, it is claimed that seven Kings were crowned. It may well have been so. Five at least of these Coronations are duly authenticated as having taken place at "Cingestune," and the custom of inaugurating a King by placing him on a sacred stone was widespread and goes back to very remote times. But as the Kings of the West Saxons and their successors gradually extended their sway over the whole of England it was expediency rather than custom which seems to have determined the choice of place for their Coronations, and this in the end was to be the determining factor in favour of Westminster. Thus Edgar had been crowned at Bath in 973, and Edward the Confessor at Winchester in

1043. It was, however, Westminster and not Winchester which was to become peculiarly associated with the Confessor. There he built a palace in order that he could watch over the rebuilding of the Abbey church in that place, and in that church, where he was regarded with special veneration, he was laid to rest. His immediate successor, Harold, may or may not have been crowned at Westminster —the records are conflicting—but it was natural that William the Conqueror, who above all things desired to be regarded not as a conqueror but as the legitimate successor of Edward the Confessor, should deliberately choose Westminster as the place for his own Coronation. Thereby he set a precedent, whether he meant it or not, which was followed by his own immediate successors, and the custom has continued to the present day.

The actual place of Coronation, therefore, has a history of nine hundred years behind it, but the ceremonies and rites wherewith our Sovereigns are consecrated have a history which is older still, so old, indeed, that some, at least, of them have their origins lost in the past. The Coronation Service, as it now exists, is no 20th-century service drawn up by the Archbishop of Canterbury for a special occasion. Although the pre-Conquest history of the English Coronation "Ordo," or Service, is obscure, it can at least be said that the service which will be used at the Coronation of Queen Elizabeth II descends directly from the service used by Archbishop Dunstan at the Coronation of King Edgar at Bath in 973.

During the Middle Ages four distinct forms of service for the consecration of an English King appear to have been used. They were the result of successive revisions of the service in order to bring it into conformity with the needs of the occasion or of the times. Two of these revisions, or recensions as they are called, date from pre-Conquest times. The earliest of them, of which there are two versions known as the "Leofric" and "Egbert" services, appear to date from the early 10th century. The "Egbert" service, which is now known to have no connection with Archbishop Egbert of York (732–66), is an amplified version of the "Leofric" service, and in it the ceremony of the Coronation is incorporated with the Mass. It is not at all certain that either of these services is English in origin. They were used, however, by St. Dunstan to draw up the service for Edgar's Coronation, and he took the opportunity to graft on to them many of the Coronation ceremonies in use on the continent at the time. The result of this "second recension" was to provide England with a full and elaborate rite which was to be the basis of the present service.

In this Edgar "Ordo," now almost a thousand years old, all the essential features of a modern Coronation appear in a primitive form—the Oath, the Anointing, the Investiture with Ring, Sword, Crown, Sceptre, and Rod, the Enthronement, and the Homage. It marked the completion of the process in England whereby the ancient Teutonic ceremonies of inauguration dating back to the remote past became blended with the distinctively Christian "hallowing" or anointing, and it put beyond question the right of the clergy to take a leading part in the service. Nothing, indeed, is more remarkable in the long history of the

16

This representation of the Crowning of William I at Westminster on Christmas Day, 1066, bears little evidence of the riot and fire which followed the Norman guards misunderstanding the tumultuous acclaim of the congregation during the Recognition. A page from a MS. book executed between 1470–80 in Flanders for Edward IV, now preserved in the British Museum.

Coronation Service than the way in which throughout the centuries the outcome of religious and political controversies have left their mark or have become embedded in the Coronation rite.

The coming of the Normans made little change. In all essentials the Norman Kings continued to be consecrated after the manner of their Saxon predecessors. In the first half of the 12th century, however, a third recension was made under the influence of Archbishop Anselm, in which the service was recast in order to bring it more into conformity with continental models. The order of investiture was finally settled, and from the German rite there was added a confirmation by the people of the King's election and investiture with a mantle and armill. The service remained in this form until the beginning of the 14th century when a fourth recension was made involving changes in detail, notably in the recasting of the Oath. These changes were elaborated, especially as regards the actual ceremonial procedure, at the end of the century and are embodied in the great Missal of Abbot Litlyngton and in an illuminated copy of the *Liber Regalis*, both of which are still preserved in the Library of Westminster Abbey.

This fourth recension, still in all essential features dating from before the Conquest, was to remain in use for over three hundred years. At the Coronation of James I in 1603 English took the place of Latin, but the service used was simply a translation of the *Liber Regalis*. Not until 1685 was there any considerable change. James II was a Roman Catholic, and in consequence Archbishop Sancroft was desired "to view the Forms of Divine Service used at former Coronations, and (keeping to the essentials) to abridge, as much as might be, the extreme length thereof." The result was a drastic revision. The Communion Service was omitted, many prayers were either largely re-written or omitted altogether, and the order of the ceremonies was slightly recast. Four years later at the Coronation of William and Mary still further changes were made. For the first time a King and Queen jointly shared the Throne, and the service had to be adapted to a double Coronation. But this was not all. Dr. Compton, Bishop of London, under whose direction the changes were made, wished to ensure that no Roman Catholic could in future be crowned as King. The Oath, therefore, was drastically altered to ensure that "the Protestant Religion Established by Law" was maintained, and, reverting to ancient usage, the whole service, like that for the consecration of a bishop, was again incorporated in the Communion Service. Furthermore the Crowning was made the final and principal act of investiture, and it was immediately followed by a striking innovation when the Bible was solemnly presented to the Sovereign as "the most valuable thing that this World affords."

The service thus re-modelled has remained very little altered since that date. It is only in the whole conception of its meaning and significance that there has been a change. In the 18th century the "puppet show," as Horace Walpole called it, was regarded merely as a curious but possibly necessary relic from the past. The Coronation of 1821 was held in the full tide of the Romantic Movement,

pres son regna henry le terz sun filz. lui aunz. si
fuit de. ix. aunz de age quant fuit coronez. E en sa
temps fuit la bataille de Guesham. ou fuit occys syr
Symund de munfort. e sun filz henry. e syre hugh le cec

EARLY WESTMINSTER CORONATIONS

On this page are featured three medieval Coronations at Westminster. The illustration on the left, a reproduction from a 14th-century illuminated MS., probably represents the second Crowning of Henry III, by the Archbishop of Canterbury on 17th May, 1220, since at his first Coronation at Gloucester on 28th October, 1216, by the Bishop of Winchester a plain circlet of gold was used. The King wearing a dark-blue mantle and red undergarment holds a sceptre in his right hand and a model of a church in his left. Henry III was the builder of the present Abbey, and the fact that in this picture he is holding a model of a church gives additional weight to the suggestion that the Westminster Coronation is depicted.

The illustration below, *left*, depicts the Crowning of ten-year-old Richard II in 1377. The third medieval Coronation here shown is of another boy-King, Henry VI, on 6th November, 1429. Two bishops place the crown of gold adorned with *fleurs-de-lys* on his head while other prelates and lay ministers stand on either side. This drawing is from the manuscript *John Rous' Life and Acts of Richard Beauchamp, Earl of Warwick*, written about 1460. The Earl of Warwick, "Master" of the eight-year-old King, carried him to the Abbey. Just over two years later Henry VI was crowned again in Paris.

ne filz du prince de gales fu fait roy dengle
terre ses oncles vivans.

pres celui an mil. ccc.lxxvii
cessus dit le. xvi. iour de iuiller
ensuiant richart filz de feu edou
art prince de galles qui auoit este aisne filz
du roy denglererre et auoir este mort auant

within the Abbey. Indeed some have seen in this raising up within the Hall the last relic of the old tribal custom of elevating a new chief on a shield. Furthermore it was not until the inauguration of the King's Bench had taken place that a message was sent to the prelates waiting within the Abbey. Thereupon they, accompanied by the abbot and monks of Westminster bearing the Regalia, came to the Palace to lead the King to the church "singing and chanting those anthems which are usually sung at the reception of kings."

It was thus the relic of an exceedingly interesting ceremony, and its discontinuance, even in the form which it had taken by 1821, is much to be regretted. The inauguration and solemn religious procession was in fact the proper preface to the service. But even apart from its significance the assembly of the procession in the Hall would provide a magnificent spectacle which could be witnessed by many for whom room cannot now be found within the Abbey, and it would obviate the necessity for building an ugly and pseudo-Gothic Annexe at the West End of the Abbey.

On the other hand probably no one now would seriously wish to see the Banquet revived. Picturesque and delightful as were many of the feudal services performed, and not least the spectacular entry of the King's Champion on horseback, they belonged to a long-past age. This was apparent even at the Coronation Banquet of George IV—the last to be held—which, splendid as it was, was little more than an outmoded pageant in which genuine tradition was mixed with the conception of chivalry made popular by the Waverley novels. The spectacle of the King presiding in his Crown with "his long train arranged up behind his head like a spread Peacock's tail," surrounded by the peers in their robes, and an immense throng of people some of whom were in a fancy dress specially devised as suitable for the occasion, might create an illusion of medievalism to the romantically minded, but even Sir Walter Scott was "somewhat disappointed" with the entry and challenge of the Champion when he saw it actually take place. In truth there was little substance behind the Banquet ceremonies and their discontinuance can only be deplored on antiquarian grounds.

THE CORONATION OATH OF HENRY VIII

On the left is a reproduction of the Coronation Oath of Henry VIII altered by the King after his crowning, probably with the intention of bringing the Oath into conformity with his later and altered views of his position as head of the Church. The passage re-written reads:

"the king shall swere that he shall kepe and mayntene the *lawfull* right and the libertees of olde tyme graunted by the rightuous Cristen kinges of Englond *to the holy chirche, nott preiudyciall to hys jurysdyction and dignite ryall* . . . And that he shall graunte to holde lawes and approvyd customes of the realme, and *lawfull and nott preiudiciall to hys crowne or imperiall juris(diction)*."

The words in italics are the King's additions in his own handwriting. From the Cotton MS., British Museum.

The wood-cut reproduced below is from "*A joyful medytacyon to all Englonde of the Coronacyon of our moost naturall soverayne lorde Kynge Henry the eyght,*" published in London in 1509, the year of the King's accession at the age of eighteen. It is the earliest printed contemporary illustration of an English Coronation. Henry VIII and Catherine of Aragon are seated under their family badges, the Tudor rose and the pomegranate. Bishops are about to perform the crowning ritual. Reproduced by courtesy of the University Library, Cambridge.

The portrait of Henry VIII, after Holbein, bottom left, is undated but was probably painted when the King was in his early thirties. Reproduced by permission of the National Portrait Gallery.

The Sovereign, wearing the Cap of Maintenance, with his Consort are seated in their Chairs of State at the beginning of the Service. On each side of the King are his supporting bishops—the Bishop of Durham on the right, and the Bishop of Bath and Wells on the left. On the Queen's right is the Bishop of St. Albans. Beside the King stands the Marquess of Zetland carrying the heavy two-handled Sword of State, and next to him the Earl of Cork and Orrery carrying Curtana or the Sword of Mercy. In the Royal Gallery behind may be seen the Princess Royal, Princess Margaret, Princess Elizabeth, Queen Mary, the Queen of Norway, and the Duchesses of Gloucester and Kent.

N.B.—Photographs of the Coronation of King George VI, on 12th May, 1937, illustrate Chapter 3 because apart from their interest they augment the text in describing the various acts of ritual.

3

THE CEREMONY AND RITUAL

WHEN the present Westminster Abbey was built it was designed mainly for the use of the monks of Westminster, but also to serve as a Coronation church. For this reason the Choir and Choir Stalls were placed west of the central crossing, leaving a space between the Choir and the steps leading up to the Sanctuary and the High Altar. In this central space at a Coronation, a stage or raised platform is built up to the level of the Sanctuary. On this platform, or "Theatre" as it is called, most of the Coronation Ceremony takes place. King Edward's Chair, or, as it is more usually called, the Coronation Chair, is placed facing the Altar midway between the two great pillars just at the top of what would normally be the Altar steps. Nearby on the south side of the Sanctuary is the Chair of State occupied by the Sovereign at the beginning of the Service. Behind the Coronation Chair on five raised steps in the centre of the Theatre is placed the Throne. The Chair of State and the Throne are specially designed afresh for each Coronation and originally the Throne was elevated even higher than it is at present. The old name for the Theatre was the Mount or Scaffold, and the Throne seems sometimes to have been placed on a kind of bridge in the middle of it with fifteen or twenty steps leading up to it. It was on some such erection that the boy King Henry VI at his Coronation is described as sitting in his seat "in the midst of the scaffold there beholding the people all about sadly and wisely."

From the 17th century to the present day the appearance of the Theatre at a Coronation has altered hardly at all. For the Coronation of Queen Elizabeth II the arrangement of the Theatre as now outlined, and the Order of the Service as described later are likely to be followed except in points of detail. On the south side of the Sanctuary is the Royal Gallery, in which are seated members of the Royal Family; opposite to them on the north side are seated the bishops. The Great Officers of State, the Heralds, the Lord Chancellor, the Lord Mayor of London, and others not in direct attendance on the Sovereign are grouped round the pillars at the four corners of the Theatre. On the right of the Throne, in the South Transept, are the peers in their robes with the Royal Princes in front of them, and opposite in the North Transept are the peeresses. In the Choir are the Royal guests, the representatives of foreign states and the

Prime Ministers and other representatives of the British Commonwealth of Nations.

Early on the morning of the Coronation the Regalia, which had been left in charge of the Dean of Westminster during the preceding night, is carried in procession by the Abbey clergy from the Jerusalem Chamber through the South and East Cloisters to the Theatre and High Altar. It is accompanied by the choirs of Westminster and the Chapel Royal, and by the Queen's Scholars of Westminster School. The Imperial State Crown is placed upon the Altar in St. Edward's Chapel, and the oil in the Ampulla is consecrated and subsequently placed on the High Altar. The rest of the Regalia is then carried in procession through the Choir to the West Door where it is delivered by the dean to the Lord Great Chamberlain to await the arrival of the Sovereign. During this procession the Litany is sung.

The Coronation Service itself may be divided into five different parts :

(1) The Introduction (*i.e.* first the Recognition and then the Oath)
(2) The Anointing
(3) The Investment with the Royal Robes and the Insignia culminating in the Crowning
(4) The Enthroning and the Homage
(5) The Celebration of the Holy Communion.

On the arrival of the Sovereign at Westminster Abbey the great Procession, which has been marshalled in the built-on Annexe by the West Door, begins to move up the Nave and Choir while the choir sing the anthem "I was glad," etc. (from Psalm cxxii). This anthem has been sung at the entry into the church since the Coronation of Charles I. It is now sung to the fine setting by the late Sir Hubert Parry.

The Procession is led by the Royal chaplains followed by the representatives of the Free Churches and of the Church of Scotland and the dean and prebendaries of Westminster. Then after the Pursuivants of the College of Arms come the Officers of the Orders of Knighthood followed by the Standard Bearers and the four Knights of the Garter appointed to hold the Canopy for the Queen's Anointing. After these come the Lord President of the Council, the Prime Minister and the Prime Ministers of the Commonwealth, the Lord Chancellor, and the Archbishops of Canterbury and York. At the last Coronation the Queen's Regalia and the Queen Consort followed, and it is probable that at this Coronation the Duke of Edinburgh will occupy this position in the Procession. Next come the bearers of the Regalia and the State Swords, the Kings of Arms, the Lord Mayor of London, and the Great Officers of State, St. Edward's Crown being carried by the Lord High Steward. Immediately behind follow three bishops carrying the Bible, the Paten, and the Chalice. Lastly comes the Queen Regnant, with her supporting bishops, surrounded and followed by the Gentlemen at Arms and the Yeoman of the Guard. It is interesting to note that the

This photograph shows the Sovereign standing bareheaded by the Coronation Chair, attended by his Pages, during the ritual of the Recognition. As the Archbishop, with the Great Officers of State, goes to each of the four corners of the Theatre presenting the Sovereign to the people as "your undoubted King," the Sovereign faces each corner in turn. In the background are the four nobles carrving the Swords. The Dean of Westminster stands by the High Altar, which is vested with the Coronation Frontal given by the Sovereign. By his side is the Treasurer of the Royal Household with his white staff of office.

general form of the Procession with the clergy leading followed by peers carrying the Swords and the Regalia is at least as ancient as the Coronation of Richard I in 1189 when William de Mandeville, Earl of Albemarle carried "a golden crown great and heavy, and adorned on all sides with precious stones" immediately in front of the King.

As the Queen emerges from beneath the Organ Loft she is greeted by the shouts of the Queen's Scholars of Westminster School—*Vivat Regina Elizabetha! Vivat! Vivat! Vivat!* This is the only Latin now used in the Service, and the privilege of being the first to acclaim the Sovereign has been exercised by the Westminster boys certainly for the last twelve Coronations.

So the Procession passes through the Choir to the raised platform or Theatre, between Choir and Altar, and the Queen takes her seat on the south side of the Sanctuary. Immediately she has done so, and at the conclusion of the anthem, the Archbishop of Canterbury, accompanied by the great Officers of State and by Garter King of Arms, goes in turn to the four corners of the Theatre and at each corner presents to the people :

Queen Elizabeth, your undoubted Queen: Wherefore All you who are come this day to do your Homage and Service, Are you willing to do the same?

The people then make reply "GOD SAVE QUEEN ELIZABETH." The Queen meanwhile stands in full view by the Coronation Chair, facing each side in turn. Formerly the Sovereign merely stood by the Chair of State on the south side of the Sanctuary, but King George V advanced and stood by the Coronation Chair, and this precedent has since been followed.

The Recognition, as it is called, is a survival from the past, for it preserves the ancient form of the ratification by the people of the election of the Sovereign. It is in fact a kind of "banns of marriage," for in theory, opportunity is given for dissent. It contrasts, therefore, with the shouts of the Westminster boys which represent the spontaneous recognition of their Sovereign by the people.

The formal Recognition is followed by the administration of the Oath, which is put to the Queen in a series of questions by the Archbishop. By this she promises to govern her peoples according to the laws of the land and to uphold the Protestant Faith. The Queen then goes to the Altar and, kneeling there, lays her hand on the Bible and swears to perform and keep the Oath which she has promised. She signs it, and returning to her chair she repeats and also signs the Declaration prescribed by Act of Parliament. The wording of the Oath has been altered from time to time and will probably be altered again to bring it into conformity with modern conditions, but by this act of dedication the Sovereign makes and signs, in the sight of all, the most solemn promises which anyone can make. It has been called "the nearest approach in the Constitution to an express fundamental contract between ruler and ruled." It is not until these promises have been made that the Sovereign can be consecrated. This completes what may be called the introductory part of the Service.

28

The Sovereign, with his supporting bishops on each side of him, is seated in King Edward's Chair immediately before the Anointing. In front of him stands Lord Zetland carrying the Sword of State. Four Knights of the Garter are bringing forward the Canopy which they hold over the Sovereign during the Anointing. The bishops are in the immediate foreground. In the photograph below, *left*, the Canopy, is above the Chair and the Archbishop is performing the ancient Anointing ritual. For the Girding of the Sword the Sovereign, clothed in the *Colobium Sindonis* and the Supertunica, or Close Pall of Cloth of Gold, stands in front of King Edward's Chair. As seen below, *right*, the Sword has been brought from the Altar and is girded about the Sovereign by the Lord Great Chamberlain. The two Archbishops stand immediately in front of the Sovereign.

The Communion Service now begins, and at once the atmosphere changes to one of devotion and deep religious significance, for it is from this point that the Sovereign, having dedicated herself to the service of her peoples, is solemnly consecrated, like a bishop, for her task. It is fitting, therefore, that after the choir has sung the hymn *Veni Creator* ("Come, Holy Ghost, our souls inspire") the Anointing should follow. This is really the central part of the Service—the most sacred and mystical part of the rite—the hallowing of the Sovereign by anointing instead of, as in the case of bishops, the imposition of hands. The exact spiritual significance of the Anointing—whether in fact by virtue of it the Sovereign acquired some kind of priestly authority—was a matter of dispute throughout the Middle Ages. The controversy has receded into the past, but the fact remains that as the Anointing in one sense sets the Sovereign apart so in another it makes the Sovereign the consecrated head of the Commonwealth. It is, too, only because the Sovereign has been thus anointed that she can be invested with the Royal Insignia culminating with the Crown.

The Queen, therefore, having discarded her Robes of State now moves to the Coronation Chair facing the Altar, in which she sits and over which four Knights of the Garter hold a canopy, for the Anointing was originally supposed to take place in secret. Meanwhile the choir sing, as they have sung at this point in the Ceremony since the earliest-known English Coronation Service, the anthem "Zadok the Priest" (now, and since the Coronation of George II, to the setting by Handel). The Archbishop, assisted by the Dean of Westminster, anoints the Queen on the hands, the breast, and the crown of the head—Queen Victoria was anointed only on the hands and head—the Archbishop saying:

> *And as Solomon was anointed King by Zadok the priest and Nathan the prophet, so be you anointed, blessed and consecrated Queen over the Peoples, whom the Lord your God hath given you to rule and govern. . . .*

At this point a King is invested first with a sleeveless garment, corresponding to a bishop's rochet, known as the *Colobium Sindonis*, and then with the sleeved *Supertunica* or *Close Pall* of cloth of gold lined with crimson silk, together with its girdle or sword belt. It is curious, however, that although these garments were certainly worn both by Queen Anne and by Queen Victoria, there is no mention of them in the rubrics of their Coronation Services. Queen Victoria, however, tells us in her *Journal* that immediately *before* the Anointing she retired to St. Edward's Chapel and "put on the supertunica of cloth of gold, in the shape of a kirtle, which was put over a singular sort of little gown of linen trimmed with lace."

The Spurs are then brought from the Altar, and in the case of a Queen Regnant, instead of the heels being touched with them, she merely touches them with her hand and they are then taken back to the Altar.

After this the Archbishop receives the Sovereign's sword and after laying it on the Altar he, assisted by other bishops, places it in the Queen's right hand,

The Sovereign, clothed in the cloth of gold Supertunica, advances from the Coronation Chair, and offers the Sword in its scabbard, with which he has just been girded, to the Dean of Westminster who places it upon the Altar. It is then redeemed for a hundred shillings and carried naked before the Sovereign for the rest of the Service. In the lower photograph the Sovereign has just been invested with the Royal Robe of cloth of gold in which he is crowned, and stands facing the Archbishop of Canterbury. The clasps have been fastened by the Lord Great Chamberlain, and now follows the delivery of the Regalia.

thereby showing that it is not delivered to her as head of the armed forces but to:

Do justice, stop the growth of iniquity, protect the Holy Church of God, help and defend widows and orphans, restore the things which are gone to decay, maintain the things that are restored, punish and reform what is amiss, and confirm what is in good order.

If the precedent of Queen Victoria's Coronation is followed the Queen, unlike a King, is not actually girded with it, but rising immediately, goes alone to the Altar where, by a beautiful act of symbolism, she offers it in the service of God. The rubric in the 14th-century *Liber Regalis* states that immediately after this "the earl who is greatest of those present shall redeem it, and then carry it naked before the king. The price of the sword belongs to the Altar." Accordingly to this day the Lord who up to this point has been carrying the Sword of State now exchanges it for the Queen's sword, which he redeems from the Altar for a hundred new shillings from the Dean of Westminster, and drawing it from its scabbard carries it for the remainder of the Service.

The Queen meanwhile has returned to the Coronation Chair where she is then invested with the *Armill*, a kind of stole, and then with the Robe Royal or Pall of cloth of gold, which is buckled in front like a cope. All these Royal robes bear so close a resemblance to ecclesiastical vestments that it was not unnatural that in medieval times they should have been confused with them and held to have been ecclesiastical in their origin. There are, however, difficulties in this theory, and it is at least as probable that their origin is really secular and is to be found in the imperial robes of the Byzantine emperors. It may well be that the Robe Royal, which is a square mantle not unlike a shawl, derives from the imperial cloak of the emperors which was worn fastened on the right shoulder by a brooch. In this form it appears on the effigy of Henry III on his tomb in the Abbey. In the same way the *Armill* may derive from the *lorum*, a broad strip of material which the emperors wore round their necks, and so not be a stole at all.

The Sovereign has now received all the Royal vestments and there follows the delivery of the Regalia, each with its own significance. First the Orb, the symbol of independent Sovereignty under the Cross; the Archbishop saying as he places it in her hand:

And when you see this Orb thus set under the Cross, remember that the whole world is subject to the Power and Empire of Christ our Redeemer.

The Orb is now a globe surmounted by a jewelled cross, but in medieval times it was a kind of sceptre; the cross surmounting a stem or staff which rose from the globe. In course of time, however, this early form of the Orb was forgotten, with the result that the Sovereign has now, rather awkwardly, to give the Orb

The supreme moment of the Coronation. The Dean of Westminster brings the Crown of St. Edward from the High Altar on a cushion from which the Archbishop takes it (*bottom, left*). Holding the Crown above the Sovereign, who is seated in the Coronation Chair, the Archbishop pauses for a moment and then reverently places it upon the King's head.

In the foreground of the photograph above are the Dean of Westminster, who is carrying the cushion from which the Crown has been taken, the Archbishop of York, the Bishop of London, and other bishops. The Queen watches the scene from her Chair of State surrounded by her Train Bearers. The peers and the Kings of Arms are about to put on their coronets.

Altar, in the centre of the Theatre. There, to quote the words of the rubric, she is :

> . . . *lifted up into it by the Archbishop and Bishops and other Peers* and solemnly *inthronised or placed therein.*

Historically this is the moment when the Sovereign enters into and takes possession of her kingdom.

The Archbishop then, in words which have come down to us almost unaltered from at least the time of William the Conqueror, charges the Queen to :

> *Stand firm, and hold fast from henceforth the Seat and State of Royal and Imperial Dignity, which is this day delivered unto you, in the name and by the authority of Almighty God, and by the hands of us the Bishops and servants of God, though unworthy.*

The Queen has been Anointed and Crowned; and now Enthroned in the sight of all she is in a position to receive the Homage of the Princes and peers. In former days the Royal Princes and the spiritual and temporal peers each did their Homage in person, but in 1902 the precedent was set, which has since been followed, that only the senior peer of each degree should kneel before the Sovereign and do the actual Homage, the rest of the peers merely kneeling in their places and repeating the words after their respective leaders. First, then,

Continued on page 38

The Fealty of the Spiritual Peers. The Archbishop of Canterbury (*centre*), the Bishop of Durham (*left*) and the Bishop of Bath and Wells (*right*) swearing to be "faithful and true" to the Sovereign.

The Sovereign and his Consort seated on their Thrones immediately after the Coronation of the Queen. They are surrounded by their Supporting Bishops, the Great Officers of State and others. In the group can be seen (behind the Thrones) the Lord Chancellor (the late Lord Hailsham), and the Lord President of the Council (the late Mr. Ramsay MacDonald). The Mistress of the Robes (the Dowager Duchess of Northumberland) stands immediately behind the Queen's Throne.

Below: The late Duke of Kent doing Homage to his brother, the King. In the group from left to right can be seen Lord Trenchard, Lord Milne, Lord Cork, Lord Zetland carrying the King's Sword, and the Dukes of Somerset and Richmond.

comes the Fealty of the archbishops and the spiritual peers. The Archbishop of Canterbury swears that he and the other spiritual peers will be "faithful and true," and, in the case of a Queen Regnant, kisses—the practice seems to have varied—either her left cheek or her hand. He is followed by the Princes of the Blood Royal, and then by the peers, who remove their coronets and do their Homage by touching the Crown and swearing to be:

Your Liege man of Life and Limb, and of earthly worship; and Faith and Truth I will bear unto you, to live and die, against all manner of Folks.

It is interesting to note that Queen Victoria was unmarried at the time of her Coronation, but that at the Coronation of Queen Anne her husband, Prince George of Denmark, seems to have done Homage before the Lords Spiritual, thus breaking the hitherto unbroken custom that the first to do Fealty and Homage should be the Archbishop of Canterbury. Although in the Service it is called Homage the archbishops and bishops actually do Fealty inasmuch as originally they held their lands in the name of the Church. They do their act of Homage, therefore, as the first estate of the realm and not as holders of baronies and, therefore, take precedence of the temporal peers.

When the Homage of the Lords Spiritual and Lords Temporal is ended, "the Drums shall beat, and the Trumpets sound, and all the people shout, crying out:

GOD SAVE QUEEN ELIZABETH.
LONG LIVE QUEEN ELIZABETH.
MAY THE QUEEN LIVE FOR EVER!"

By this threefold acclamation, which is of great antiquity, the people present, representing the third estate, complete the act of Homage and thus end the solemnity of the Sovereign's Coronation.

In the case of a King Regnant the Coronation of the Queen Consort immediately follows, otherwise the Service of the Holy Communion is resumed at the Offertory. The Queen goes to the Altar where she offers Bread and Wine, a curious survival of primitive practice, and makes her personal Oblation which takes the form of "an Ingot or Wedge of Gold of a pound weight," and, at the last three Coronations "a Pall or Altar Cloth." She then removes her Crown and kneels at a faldstool placed in front of the Altar while the Service proceeds.

After the final Blessing, the choir, since 1902, have sung a solemn and triumphant *Te Deum*. Meanwhile the Queen, who returned to her Throne after making her Communion and is now wearing the Imperial State Crown in place of St. Edward's Crown, descends and passes through the Altar Screen to St. Edward's Chapel beyond during what is known as the Recess. There, in her Traverse, she is disrobed of her Royal Robe of State and arrayed in her Robe of Purple Velvet. Then the Procession having been marshalled, the Queen wearing her Crown and carrying the Sceptre with the Cross and the Orb, passes from the Altar through the Choir to the West Door of the Abbey.

The Sovereign, crowned and carrying the Sceptre with the Cross and the Orb, with his Supporting Bishops and his Pages, and escorted by the Honourable Corps of Gentlemen at Arms, proceeds towards the West Door of the Abbey. In front are the Lord High Steward (The Marquess of Salisbury), the Duke of Sutherland and the Duke of Richmond. Behind follows the Master of the Horse (The Duke of Beaufort) with the Vice-Admiral of the United Kingdom and the Gold Stick in Waiting.

The Most Reverend and Right Honourable The Archbishop of Canterbury (Dr. Geoffrey Francis Fisher), who, as Primate of All England, will crown the Queen. Dr. Fisher was formerly Headmaster of Repton School. In 1932 he was appointed Bishop of Chester, and in 1939 he became Bishop of London. In 1945 he succeeded Dr. Temple as Archbishop of Canterbury. Dr. Fisher is Prelate of the Order of the British Empire, and Bailiff Grand Cross of the Order of St. John of Jerusalem. He also holds the Royal Victorian Chain. In this photograph he is vested in Cope and Mitre and is holding the Primatial Cross of Canterbury.

4

DIGNITARIES AT THE CEREMONY

N the weeks before a modern Coronation a number of rehearsals take place during which those who play the principal parts work out the details of the complicated ceremonial. It may, therefore, be of interest to describe some of the more important duties which are carried out by those who take part in the Service.

After the Sovereign the most important person present is the Archbishop of Canterbury. He has the duty not only of preparing the Service and of making such verbal or other alterations as may be necessary, but to him alone belongs the right of conducting the Service and of anointing and crowning the Sovereign. The right of the Archbishop to crown the Sovereign was established with the greatest difficulty in medieval times owing to the traditional rivalry between the Archbishops of Canterbury and York. There was the further difficulty which arose if, for any reason, the Archbishop was prevented from attending, or if the See of Canterbury happened to be vacant. Tradition, however, and the fact that Westminster became the recognised place of Coronation favoured the claims of Canterbury, and his right to officiate was confirmed by the Pope at the end of the 12th century. When in 1216 it was necessary to crown the young Henry III hurriedly at Gloucester, in the absence of the Archbishop of Canterbury abroad, it was neither the Papal Legate nor the Archbishop of York who officiated but the Bishop of Winchester as suffragan of Canterbury. Even so the Legate felt it necessary to explain both to the Archbishop of Canterbury and to the Abbot of Westminster (where his letter has been preserved among the Muniments of the Abbey) that the proceedings had been dictated by the necessities of the time and without prejudice to their rights. Four years later a second Coronation took place at Westminster when King Henry was duly anointed by the Archbishop of Canterbury, and thenceforth his right to officiate, either in person or by deputy, was undisputed. The only exceptions since that time have been that for various special reasons Edward II and Mary I were crowned by the Bishop of Winchester of the time, Elizabeth I by the Bishop of Carlisle (Oglethorpe), and William III and Mary II by the Bishop of London (Compton). At all other Coronations the Sovereign has been crowned by the Archbishop of Canterbury.

The Archbishop of York, therefore, has no special part in the Ceremony, except that he is one of those who stands in immediate proximity to the Sovereign at the actual Crowning, and that he and others bring the Bible from the Altar for presentation immediately afterwards. It is often said that the Archbishop of York has the right to crown a Queen Consort. But this is not so, and it was only owing to the age and infirmity of Dr. Temple, then Archbishop of Canterbury, that the Archbishop of York (Maclagan) crowned Queen Alexandra in 1902. At the Coronation of King George V in 1911 the Sermon (omitted in 1937) was preached by Dr. Lang, then the northern Primate.

Two other bishops take a special part in the Ceremony. Since the Coronation of Richard I in 1189 the Bishops of Durham and of Bath (and Wells) have had the right to "support" the Sovereign, and to stand immediately on his or her right and left throughout the Service. It is a curious instance of the persistence of tradition. It arose from the fact that in 1189 these two happened to be the senior bishops. Nevertheless the right of the holders of these Sees to perform this duty has never since been disputed. A Queen Consort also has supporting bishops, but she has the right to appoint whom she pleases for this duty.

After the Archbishop of Canterbury, the Dean of Westminster has a leading part to play in a Coronation. As the successor of the Abbots of Westminster he claims the right to instruct the Sovereign on all matters connected with the Ceremony. He assists the Archbishop by holding the Ampulla at the Anointing, and by pouring the oil from it into the Anointing Spoon. He also receives the Royal insignia during the investiture and gives them to the Archbishop as required. Finally it is from him that the Archbishop takes the Crown and places it on the Sovereign's head. In former days the Abbot and Convent of Westminster, and afterwards their successors, the Dean and Chapter of Westminster, claimed and received as their right everything which was brought into the church for a Coronation. The claim is still made and until 1937 was still set out both in English and in French. It includes such things as the thrones, chairs, cushions and carpets, all the oblations and offerings, the poles of the Canopy "and the four little bells that hang at each corner," and "an hundred manchets (loaves) the third part of a tun of Wine, and Fish . . . for the Dean and Chapter's Repast on the Coronation Day." The claim is allowed by the Court of Claims, but compensation is now paid in lieu of the actual articles claimed.

The most important lay officer is the Earl Marshal. He is in charge of all the arrangements for a Coronation. He issues the invitations, makes all necessary regulations, appoints the Gold Staffs who act as stewards, and is in sole control of the Abbey on the actual day. As head of the College of Arms he is assisted by Garter Principal King of Arms, whose duty it is to marshal the processions and regulate the ceremonies, and by the Heralds and Pursuivants. Apart from these duties the Earl Marshal takes little personal part in the actual Service, but he accompanies the Great Officers of State and the Archbishop to the four corners of the Theatre at the Recognition and assists at the Inthronisation.

The office of Lord Great Chamberlain, like that of the Earl Marshal, is

The Very Reverend The Dean of Westminster (Dr. Alan Campbell Don, K.C.V.O.) who by virtue of his office plays a leading part in the Coronation Service. He is wearing one of the embroidered crimson copes which were made for the Abbey clergy for the Coronation of King Charles II. Dr. Don was formerly Chaplain to the Archbishop of Canterbury (Dr. Lang) and carried the Primatial Cross at the Coronation of King George VI. He was appointed Dean of Westminster in 1946.

hereditary and is held at present by the Marquess of Cholmondeley. He is in charge of the Palace of Westminster, but since the ceremonies in Westminster Hall were discontinued his duties have decreased. It was formerly his duty to dress the Sovereign on the morning of the Coronation, and if, as was at one time usual, the Sovereign had spent the night at the Palace of Westminster, the Lord Great Chamberlain could claim the bed in which he had slept as a perquisite, and also the furniture of the room. He is still in close attendance during the Service, and it is his duty to robe and disrobe the Sovereign as required at various parts of the Service. At the Coronation of a King it is he who touches the King's heels with the Spurs and girds him with the Sword.

The duties of the Lord High Constable have also decreased in importance. He and the Earl Marshal formerly rode together in the procession from the Tower, and they accompanied on horseback the King's Champion when he rode into Westminster Hall at the Banquet. The office is not now hereditary, and both he and the Lord High Steward, whose privilege it is to carry St. Edward's Crown in the Procession, are appointed at each Coronation. They are both Great Officers of State and take part in the Recognition and Inthronisation.

Five peers have a special duty to perform at the Homage. Immediately after the Royal Princes, the Duke of Norfolk, the Marquess of Winchester, the Earl of Shrewsbury, Viscount Hereford, and Lord de Ros, as the holders of the senior creations in each degree, do personal Homage to the Sovereign on behalf of the rest of the peerage. At the Coronation of King George VI, as the Marquess of Winchester was unable to be present the Marquess of Huntly, the Premier Marquess of Scotland, did Homage for that degree, and Lord Mowbray, as premier baron, took the place of the holder of the premier barony, the Baroness de Ros.

In medieval times the tenure of a Manor by virtue of rendering some personal service to the King was not uncommon. Such tenures, by grand sergeanty as it was called, were abolished in the 17th century, but the actual service continues to be rendered in two notable instances at a Coronation. It is by virtue of holding the Manor of Scrivelsby that the head of the Dymoke family claims to be the King's Champion, and is now allowed to carry one of the two Standards in the Procession within the Abbey. In the same way it is the privilege of the Lord of the Manor of Worksop to provide a glove for the Sovereign's right hand and to support the Sovereign's right arm "as occasion may require." This curious survival of an ancient right was duly performed at the last Coronation by the Earl of Lincoln (acting as deputy for his father, the Duke of Newcastle, who was Lord of the Manor). The glove was presented and put on immediately before the Sceptre with the Cross was placed in the King's right hand.

Even more ancient is the claim of the Barons of the Cinque Ports to carry the Canopy over the Sovereign at a Coronation. It was described as "an ancient custom" at the Coronation of Richard I in 1189. The Canopy was carried over the King from Westminster Hall to the West Door of the Abbey. At the Coronation

THE EARL MARSHAL

Bernard Marmaduke Fitzalan-Howard, sixteenth Duke of Norfolk, holds the hereditary office of Earl Marshal of England, and as such is, under the Sovereign, the highest authority on all matters of Royal ceremonial, precedence, armorial bearings, and dignities. He superintends the arrangements for the Coronation, with the exception of church liturgy in the Abbey, being responsible for the sending out of all invitations and summonses to attend; for the period of preparation for the Coronation he has special authority over Westminster Abbey.

The office of Earl Marshal has evolved from that of Marshal of England, which was one of the five great offices of state. The first Marshal of whom there is a record was a certain Gilbert, whose descendants assumed the surname of Marshal from their office. It later passed from them to the Bigods and to the Mowbrays, Dukes of Norfolk (one of which first bore the office of *Earl* Marshal in 1386), and then to the Howards, but it did not become strictly hereditary in that family until 1674, when Charles II conferred it on Henry Howard, Earl of Norwich (who later became Duke of Norfolk) and his heirs.

As *ex-officio* head of the College of Arms, the Earl Marshal largely delegates his authority to Garter, the Principal King of Arms, who is his deputy and executive officer. He used to preside over the Court of Chivalry, and to try those who infringed heraldic regulations. Although the last case was brought as long ago as 1735, the Earl Marshal could probably still adjudicate on an armorial dispute, if it was brought, for the Court has never been abolished.

The College of Arms was incorporated by Richard III in 1484, and the present premises were granted by charter of Queen Mary Tudor. Although the original house was burnt down in the Great Fire of London in 1666, when mercifully the records were saved, the present building was built on the same site.

GARTER KING OF ARMS

The historic office of Garter King of Arms, which was instituted by Henry V in 1415, is now held by the Hon. Sir George R. Bellew, C.V.O. As the title of his office shows, he is King of Arms of the Most Noble Order of the Garter, and as such conducts the ceremonies and attends upon the Knights at their Installation in St. George's Chapel, Windsor, and at other ceremonies connected with that oldest order of chivalry in the world.

Among his other principal duties is the running of the College of Arms. Armorial bearings are here granted and pedigrees prepared and recorded.

Garter and the other officers of Arms have many ceremonial duties such as the reading of Royal Proclamations, the marshalling of state ceremonies, and official attendance at the Opening of Parliament; and as the principal lieutenant of the Earl Marshal his busiest time is in the planning of the elaborate ceremonial of the Coronation.

His tabard is of gold and velvet like those of the provincial Kings of Arms, but he alone has also a crimson satin mantle which he wears as an Officer of the Order of the Garter. In the photograph taken before Sir George became King of Arms, he wears the tabard of a Herald.

of James II Samuel Pepys was one of the bearers. The custom continued down to and including the Coronation of George IV. With the discontinuance of the procession from the Hall the Canopy was no longer required, but the right of the barons to bear it, should it be the Sovereign's pleasure to have a canopy, has been preserved. In their picturesque Tudor dress they are still in attendance at a Coronation. They are now grouped at the entrance to the Choir, where the Standards carried in the Procession are handed to them by those appointed to bear them. They hold the Standards during the Service and return them to the bearers as the Procession passes out at the conclusion of the Service.

The Sovereign's Supporting Bishops. The Right Reverend The Lord Bishop of Bath and Wells (Dr. Harold William Bradfield) (*left*), and The Right Reverend The Lord Bishop of Durham (Dr. Arthur Michael Ramsey). The portraits are by Cyril Howe and Daisy E. Edis, F.R.P.S., F.I.B.P. respectively.

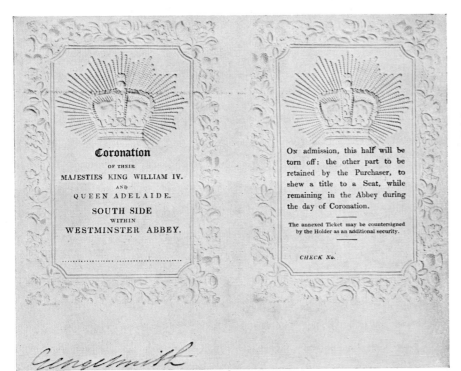

Coronation
OF THEIR
MAJESTIES KING WILLIAM IV.
AND
QUEEN ADELAIDE.

SOUTH SIDE
WITHIN
WESTMINSTER ABBEY.

On admission, this half will be torn off: the other part to be retained by the Purchaser, to shew a title to a Seat, while remaining in the Abbey during the day of Coronation.

The annexed Ticket may be countersigned by the Holder as an additional security.

CHECK No.

CORONATION TICKETS

The Coronations of the Hanoverian Kings of England are notable for the emphasis laid on the secular rather than on the spiritual aspect. The Ceremony in the Abbey was staged more as a splendid entertainment than a deeply religious service, and seats were frequently sold by Court officials, and, on occasion, by the prebendaries of Westminster. The inscription on the ticket for an Abbey view of William IV's crowning (*left*) quite blatantly refers to the "purchaser."

The design of the 1831 Coronation ticket is poor compared with the earlier examples. That for the Ceremony of George III (*bottom, right*) is finely designed and engraved, and the ticket which entitled the holder to watch George IV's magnificent progress from the Abbey to Westminster Hall (*centre, left*) displays the elegance always associated with the First Gentleman. Other examples of Coronation tickets illustrated are George III (*bottom, left*) and George IV (*centre, right*).

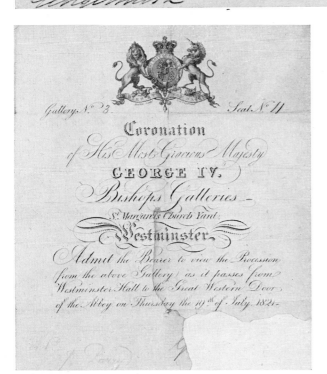

Gallery No. 3.　　　Seat No. 11.

Coronation
of His Most Gracious Majesty
GEORGE IV.
Bishops Galleries
St Margaret's Church Yard
Westminster

Admit the Bearer to view the Procession from the above Gallery as it passes from Westminster Hall to the Great Western Door of the Abbey on Thursday the 19th of July 1821.

Coronation Ticket WESTMINSTER ABBEY Sep.r 22: 1761.

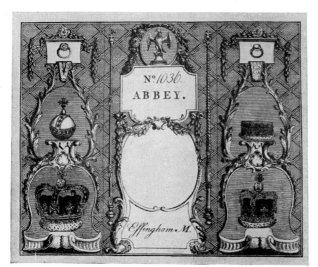

No. 1036.
ABBEY.

Effingham M.

47

feru si auoit ce este par male ad
uenture et non pouoir aussi sen
alla en northmandie a saincte.
Et de la ou chastel de chaumont

ou il demoura depuis longue
ment Si sauons a parler de luy
ancois retournerons dutout
au texte de nostre matiere.

Sensieut le couronnement du roy
henry frere du roy guillaume le
rouz Chappitre · [...] vujme
[O] Il commence listore
du roy henry dans/
leterre frere du roy
guillaume le rouz enffant du
roy guillamme le bastart laquel
parle premiers de son couronne
ment Et puis comment il espou
sa la fille du roy descoce apres la
mort du roy rouz lequel apres
quil eut regne xiii ans et siv.
semptmaines morut par la ma

mere qui seurement aues ouy
ou chappitre precedent · [...] Or
donques apres la mort du roy
rouz les prelatz et barons danj/
leterre sassamblerent a conseil
ou ilz concluxent que henry fre/
re dudit roy rouz serut enomt
et couronne roy De laquelle cho/
se henry sexcusa moult fort en
disant que ceste honneur appar
tenoit au ducq robert de northy/
mendie son frere qui estoit
oultre mer Car il estoit laisne
mais tres uoulentiers apdeuit

The Coronation of Henry I at Westminster in 1100. On the left of the illustration an archbishop is placing the Crown on the King's head, a noble on his knees holds a Sceptre whilst another holds a flagon which presumably held the Holy Oil for the Anointing. Through the window the Coronation Banquet is seen: the King with his Queen, Matilda, are seated at a table. One attendant offers the King a covered cup, another attendant proffers a bowl. From a 15th-century MS.

5

SOME MEDIEVAL CORONATIONS

I N a letter to the Abbot of Fécamp some ten years after the Conquest, William the Conqueror, who was about to appoint a new Abbot of Westminster, tells him that he has that Abbey "and indeed ought to have it, in the greatest veneration. For here lies my lord King Edward of blessed memory: there too has been buried Queen Edith his noble wife: and there, by God's merciful providence I received the sceptre and crown of all England."

He was indeed unlikely to have forgotten the dramatic scenes of that memorable day. They have been told inimitably by Dean Stanley:

"'Two nations were indeed in the womb' of the Abbey on that day. Within the massive freshly-erected walls was the Saxon populace of London, intermixed with the retainers of the Norman camp and court. Outside sate the Norman soldiers on their war-horses, eagerly watching for any disturbance in the interior. . . . Before the high altar, standing on the very gravestone of Edward, was the fierce, huge, unwieldy William, the exact contrast of the sensitive transparent King who lay beneath his feet. On either side stood an Anglo-Saxon and a Norman prelate. . . . The moment arrived for the ancient form of popular election. The Norman prelate was to address in French those who could not speak English; the Saxon primate was to address in English those who could not speak French. A confused acclamation arose from the mixed multitude. The Norman cavalry without, hearing but not understanding this peculiarity of the Saxon institution, took alarm, and set fire to the gates of the Abbey, and perhaps the thatched dwellings which surrounded it. The crowd—nobles and poor, men and women—alarmed in their turn, rushed out. The prelates and monks were left alone with William in the church, and in the solitude of that wintry day, amidst the cries of his new subjects, trampled down by the horses' hoofs of their conquerors, he himself, for the first time in his life trembling from head to foot, the remainder of the ceremony was hurried on. Aldred Abp of York, in the name of the Saxons, exacted from him the oath to protect them before he would put the crown on his head. Thus ended the first undoubted Westminster coronation."

We may, perhaps, as a contrast take the Coronation of another warrior King just over a hundred years later, that of Richard I on 3rd September, 1189; the first for which a detailed account of the Ceremony exists, for not only is the ritual described, but the names of those who were present and took part in the Ceremony are carefully recorded.

We are told how the Duke of Normandy (as the chronicler is careful to call him until he was actually crowned) was led "with an ordered procession and triumphal chanting" from the Palace of Westminster to the Abbey, and how behind the procession "the whole crowd of earls, barons, knights, and others, clerk and lay, followed up to the door of the church and were brought with the Duke into the Choir." There, at the Altar, the Duke swore on his knees to protect the Church, exercise justice, annul evil laws, and "make good laws and keep them without fraud or evil intent." He was then anointed and clothed with the Royal vestments. The account goes on: "Then the Archbishop gave him the sword of the realm wherewith he was to repress evildoers against the Church. Then two earls put on him the spurs which John Marshal had carried. Then he was vested with the mantle. After that he was led to the altar, and there the said Archbishop forbad him by Almighty God to take this great office upon him, unless he intended to keep inviolate the oaths above mentioned and the vows he had made. And he replied that by the help of God he would keep all the above without deceit. Then he himself took the crown from the altar, and gave it to the Archbishop, and the Archbishop set it on his head, and two earls held it up on account of its weight. Then the Archbishop put the royal sceptre into his right hand and the royal rod into his left, and thus crowned the king was led to his seat, by the aforesaid Bishops of Durham and Bath, preceded by torch bearers and the said three swords." The celebration of the Mass followed, and then "the lord king laid aside his royal crown and his royal vestments, and put on lighter crowns and vestments" for the Banquet which followed in Westminster Hall.

It has been worth while to quote this contemporary account at length, for it illustrates in a striking way how little in essentials the Coronation Service has altered from that day to this. But even on this occasion the chroniclers characteristically felt bound to record the evil omens which made so great an impression on the medieval mind. Who, for instance, could fail to notice the bat which even "in the middle and bright part of the day" fluttered round the King's head, or, worse still and indeed "hardly allowable to be related even in a whisper" the mysterious and unaccountable peal of bells which broke the silence "at the last hour of the day."

In a service which took place at irregular intervals and which depended on the orderly sequence of symbolic ritual, it was perhaps inevitable that it was the abnormal which tended to be recorded and to be remembered afterwards as presaging future events. It might have been expected that the chroniclers would have recorded the fact that Edward II was the first of our Sovereigns to be seated at his Coronation in the Chair which his father had caused to be made to enclose

et autres en chappes de draps dor
brodees de perles deuant lesquelz

Cy deuise les ordonnances du sa
...au marchand dangleterre

li rois richars fu coronnez: et comment
li rois ples prist congie a S. Denys.

Pres la mort le roi henri fu
coronne: richars aiens de

THE CORONATION OF RICHARD COEUR-DE-LION

The illustration above is from an illuminated page of a late 15th-century MS. of *Les Anciennes et Nouvelles Chroniques d'Angleterre*, dedicated and presented either to Edward IV or Edward V. It purports to depict the Coronation Procession of Richard I in 1189.

The Procession is supposed to be nearing Westminster. It is led by the monks of Westminster with their abbot and a bishop, both carrying croziers. Two more bishops follow preceded by four candlebearers. Next come two nobles carrying the Sceptre with the Cross and the Sceptre with the Dove, and they are followed by the three Swords. Four nobles carry the great chest on their shoulders which contains the Royal Vestments. The Crown is borne in front of the King who is depicted with his Supporting Bishops walking beneath a Canopy held by the Barons of the Cinque Ports.

On the left of this page is a representation of the Crowning of Richard I. This also is taken from an illuminated MS. book, written in France in the second quarter of the 14th century. Two archbishops place the Crown on the King's head. To the right of the illustration a tower is wreathed in flames, depicting according to the text, the burning of Gisors in Normandy, where in 1198 Richard Coeur-de-Lion defeated Philip Augustus of France.

the Stone of Scone. They were, however, more concerned with the fact that the solemn rites had been scrambled through with indecent haste, and that the Crown had been polluted by being carried in the Procession, not by one of the greater magnates, but by the hated favourite, Piers Gaveston, who "strutted about in purple embroidered with pearls, eclipsing the very king himself."

So, too, amid all the magnificence of the Coronation of Richard II it was noted, as something more than an unfortunate incident, that when at length completely worn out by the length of the Service, the boy King was carried back in his robes to the Palace on the shoulders of Sir Simon Burley—"contrary to ancient custom, the Abbot of the place protesting"—one of the King's red velvet shoes, which had been blessed by the Pope, fell off and was never recovered.

The Coronation of Richard II was noteworthy in other ways. For the first time, Sir John Dymoke, as Lord of the Manor of Scrivelsby, asserted and maintained his right to appear fully armed as the King's Champion. He should, no doubt, have accompanied the King in the state ride from the Tower to Westminster on the evening before the Coronation and have issued his challenge at certain places on the route. Actually, however, he seems to have appeared quite unexpectedly at the West Door of the church after the Service was over, and was then rather ignominiously told to return later and proffer his services during the Banquet which followed. In truth it was unlikely that his services would ever be required, and even at that date he belonged rather to the picturesque past than to the present. None-the-less the entry of the Champion and his challenge to meet in personal combat "any person, of what degree soever, high or low" who should dispute the King's right "to the imperial crown of this realm," continued down the centuries as the most dramatic and popular feature of the Coronation Banquet and as a striking reminder of feudal service. Even today, when Banquet and Champion have receded into the past, the head of the house of Dymoke still takes his place in the Coronation Procession within the Abbey bearing one of the Standards, by the grace of the Sovereign.

The procession from the Tower, which is also first mentioned as taking place at the Coronation of Richard II, continued to be a feature of the Coronation festivities for centuries. It was at once the most magnificent and the most impressive of pageants. In 1377 the glittering cavalcade with the young Richard as the central figure—bare headed and so good looking that he was described as "a second Absalom"—took three hours to pass from the Tower to Westminster. At every turn he passed under triumphal arches and was met by pageantry and allegorical figures. At the Little Conduit, opposite Foster Lane, there was erected a castle with four turrets and a dome. In each turret was a maiden of the King's own age who blew golden leafs at him and showered florins (of imitation gold as we are carefully told!) beneath his horse's feet. Then descending they offered him wine in a golden cup, while a gilded angel in the dome leaned forward and extended to him a crown.

All this was very much in the spirit of the age. The citizens of London

A MEDIEVAL CROWNING ON THE SCAFFOLD

The representation above of the Coronation of Henry IV, from a 15th-century illuminated MS. of *Froissart's Chronicles*, shows very clearly the Throne placed on the raised "mount" or "scaffold" erected in the central space between the Choir and the Altar of Westminster Abbey. The King sits crowned in the sight of all. One prelate supports the Crown, the other places the Sceptre in the King's hand. Nobles and courtiers below the mount make a striking group, while on the steps leading to the Altar three attendants hold the King's crowned Helm, Shield of Arms, and sheathed Sword.

The illustration, *left*, is taken from an early 14th-century Norman–French version of the Coronation Service. The King is seated in what is apparently the earliest representation of the Coronation Chair. He wears the *Colobium Sindonis* with long sleeves. Over this are two tunicles, one red, the other rayed yellow and pale blue. Over all is the Royal Mantle or *Pallium* furred with ermine. The Crown is a gold circlet with jewelled fleurons. In his right hand the King holds a gold sceptre surmounted by a finial of leaves, his left hand supports a red orb with a long white cross. This is the earlier form of the Sceptre with the Cross. The Archbishop of Canterbury stands on the King's right and is steadying the Crown with his left hand. On the King's left are, probably, the Archbishop of York and the Abbot of Westminster. Nobles, judges, and courtiers stand around, one of whom holds a round piece of gold for the King to offer at the Altar. It is difficult to specify whose Coronation the picture is meant to represent, it is perhaps merely a general representation of the majesty of the Coronation Ceremony.

delighted in such shows, and they became increasingly elaborate as the years went on. They marked a phase when there was a real danger that the religious significance of the Coronation itself would be lost and become a mere incident in the pageantry, the joustings, and the festivities by which it was surrounded. In the end the prolonged celebrations proved their own undoing. "The luxuriant growth of superabundant festivities" had to be pruned, and the Service itself, partly as the result of the Reformation and partly from other causes, was gradually reduced to manageable proportions although the essential features remained unchanged.

Edward VI, son of Henry VIII and Jane Seymour, is here portrayed passing Cheapside Cross in the procession through the City of London on the eve of his Coronation in 1547. The youthful King is seen riding a white horse beneath the canopy to the left of the Cross. This illustration is an enlargement of a detail from the *Vetusta Monumenta* print, the whole of which is reproduced and described on pages 56 and 57.

THE 1559 CROWNING

Only one contemporary impression of the Coronation of Queen Elizabeth I exists. It consists of a series of pen-and-ink drawings and has only recently been acquired by the British Museum. The artist, believed to be one of the Heralds who was present, has depicted the progress through the City of London to Westminster, probably as an official record. Sections from the MS. are reproduced below. The first shows the procession leaving the Tower, and the second the Queen in her litter borne by two horses. At each of the four corners of the litter a Knight supports the Canopy, and the Queen, who wears a robe with wide sleeves and a flowing train, is carrying an unidentified piece of Regalia.

The engraving on the left of Elizabeth I seated on the King's Bench in Parliament is reproduced from Sir Simonds D'Ewes, *Compleat Journal* published in 1682.

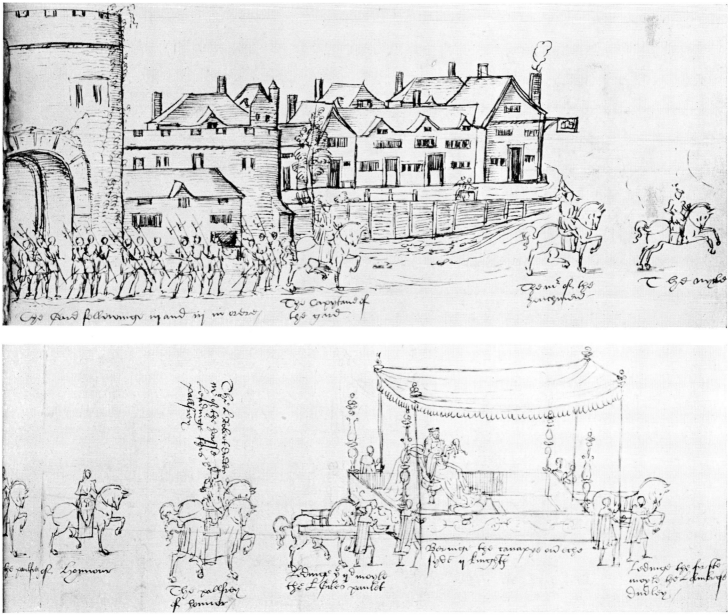

THE GREAT MEDIEVAL CORONATION PROCESSIONS

The print above from the *Vetusta Monumenta* was engraved from the original at Cowdray, Sussex, since destroyed. It depicts Edward VI in procession from the Tower of London to Westminster Palace on the eve of his Coronation in 1547. The earliest recorded procession is that of Richard II, and they continued as a customary part of the Coronation Ceremonies until dispensed with by James II in 1685. The new King progressed to Westminster in a cavalcade with an escort of Lords Temporal and accompanied through the City by the Mayor and Aldermen of the City of London, together with Heralds, Serjeants at Arms, Trumpeters, and Minstrels. These processions were essentially secular in character in which the King showed himself, usually bareheaded, to his people.

The Edward VI procession, here seen apparently in Cheapside, winds its way past old St. Paul's with its spire, along Fleet Street, through Temple Bar, and so past the palaces which lay along the Strand, to Westminster. The houses, palaces, and halls along the route are gaily decorated, carpets hang from the balconies, and the streets are lined by the Liverymen of the City Companies in their gowns, and other spectators, some of whom have climbed on the roofs in order to obtain a better view. The King rides under a canopy in the midst of the cavalcade. The Tower of London and London Bridge, appear in the background.

The picture gives a good impression of the pageantry of one of these Royal progresses. It will be noted, also, how closely the country at that time approached the southern bank of the river.

The Coronation of "Dutch William" (William III) and Mary II in Westminster Abbey naturally caused great interest among his fellow countrymen. Somewhat imaginative engravings were printed in Holland depicting the ceremonies through Dutch eyes. The illustration on the facing page, however, shows tolerably accurately the procession from Westminster Hall to the West Door of the Abbey on the morning of the Coronation.

The great nobles are shown carrying the Regalia. As William and Mary were joint Sovereigns the various emblems of the Regalia had to be doubled. These can be clearly seen in the picture. Behind the nobleman carrying the Crown are three bishops bearing the Chalice, Paten, and Bible. They are followed by the King and Queen, with their Supporting Bishops, under a Canopy upheld by the Barons of the Cinque Ports.

ALCADE or HIS MAIESTIES PASSING THROVGH THE CITY OF LONDON TOWARD.

The Duke of York

Chaplains hauing dignities, 10.   The King's Aduocate   The King's Learned   The King's puifn
The King's Remembrancer.   Masters of the Chancery.   Councel at Law.   Serjeants

The Duke of Yorke   Serjants   at   Armes

THE KING   Gentlemen Pensioners   Yeomen of the Guard   The Duke of Albemarle Master of the Horse,   The Vice Chamberlaine
Equeries   & Equeries   Leading a Horse of Estate

Charles II was crowned twice. In the parish church of Scone, as a fugitive in 1651, he received a crown from the Marquess of Argyll. On his Restoration ten years later, on 23rd April, 1661, he was crowned in Westminster Abbey. This was the last occasion when the ceremonies were enacted in full medieval splendour.

On Coronation Eve there was the customary progress from the Tower to Westminster. After a decade of repressive Puritanism the people gave vent to their feelings and received the King with joyous acclaim. Wenceslaus Hollar—once drawing master to Prince Charles—depicted the cavalcade. Sections from his *Coronation of Charles II* are reproduced above. Pepys also was there. In his *Diary* he tells us that he was up early and put on a new velvet coat in honour of the occasion. From a house in Cornhill with his friends he "saw the show very well."

Pepys describes the procession as it passed and says that "the King, in a most rich embroidered suit and cloak, looked most noble . . . the streets all gravelled, and the houses hung with carpets before them, made brave show, and the ladies out of the windows, one of which over against us I took much notice of. . . . So glorious was the show with gold and silver, that we were not able to look at it, our eyes at last being so much overcome with it. Both the King and the Duke of York took notice of us, as he saw us at the window."

On the following morning Pepys was up at four and went to the Abbey. He was disappointed to find that from his seat he could not see the ritual but "I took a great deal of pleasure to go up and down, and look upon the ladies, and to hear the music of all sorts, but above all the 24 violins."

Reproduced above are three of the many engravings from *The History of the Coronation of the Most High, Most Mighty and Most Excellent Monarch James II*, compiled by Francis Sandford, Lancaster Herald, and published in 1687. Sandford's text records the occasion in great detail. The musical part of the procession from Westminster Hall to the Abbey is described in Chapter 9.

The State Coach, in which six English Sovereigns have proceeded to their Coronations, was designed by Sir William Chambers and completed in 1762 at a total cost of £7,562 4s. 3d. The framework of the body consists of eight members representing palm trees which support the roof on which is the Royal Crown upheld by three cherubs. From four large tritons, carved by Joseph Wilton, the body of the coach is slung. The panels are painted with allegorical scenes by Cipriani, and the back wheels of the Coach, which are nearly six feet in diameter, are copied from those on an ancient triumphal car.

The print below depicts George IV, under a Canopy upheld by the Barons of the Cinque Ports, returning along the Platform through the Sanctuary to Westminster Hall for the Banquet after his Coronation in Westminster Abbey.

6

MORE HISTORIC CROWNINGS

N an earlier chapter some mention has been made of the omens and untoward happenings which the medieval chroniclers recorded as having occurred at the Coronations of those whose reigns were ultimately to close in disaster. Few Coronations were so prolific of such happenings as that of the ill-fated Charles I. It was noted that the King, who came by water from Whitehall to Westminster, was expected to have landed at Sir Robert Cotton's steps, where Sir Robert stood ready to receive him. He had in his hands the copy of the Gospels, which was said to have belonged to King Athelstan, and upon which "for divers hundred yeares together the Kings of England had solemnlie taken ther coronation oath." But the barge "bawked those stepps" and ran aground, so that "His Majestie & the Lordes were faine to use the neighbour boates for ther landing." This was only the beginning of the misfortunes of that unhappy day. The King, as some said by the unfortunate advice of Archbishop Laud, appeared in white instead of the usual purple, and it was remembered that "white was the ancient colour for a victim." At the Recognition, by some misunderstanding, there was dead silence until Lord Arundel told the people that they should cry out "God save King Charles." The preacher chose for his sermon the unfortunate text, "Be thou faithful unto death, and I will give thee a crown of life"; and finally during the Ceremony an earth tremor was felt which "did affright all in the neighbourhood."

At James II's Coronation it was the Crown itself which appeared to be about to fall off the King's head. It was steadied by Henry Sidney who remarked "This is not the first time, Your Majesty, that my family have supported the Crown." Almost at the moment of the Crowning it was noted that the Royal Standard at the Tower of London was torn asunder by the wind.

Even in the 20th century when King Edward VII's sudden operation two days before the Ceremony caused the Coronation to be postponed, there were some who recalled a prophecy that he was never destined to be crowned. The prophecy, happily, was not fulfilled, but when the Coronation eventually took place there was a terrible moment when the Crown seemed about to slip from the trembling hands of the aged Primate (Dr. Temple) before he lowered it reverently, albeit the wrong way round, on the King's head. Far otherwise and more memorable was the superbly deliberate pause made by the late Archbishop Lang as he held the Crown for a moment above the head of King George VI.

At an earlier Coronation, that of George IV, Lord Anglesey, who was carrying the Crown, allowed it to slip from its cushion but succeeded in retrieving it before it reached the ground. No one, however, who saw him later in the day as he rode up Westminster Hall during the Banquet ever forgot "the exquisite grace" and skill with which he managed his horse. At the previous Coronation in 1761 his predecessor as Lord High Steward, Lord Talbot, was less adroit. "Lord Talbot," wrote Horace Walpole, who was a spectator, "piqued himself on backing his horse down the Hall, and not turning its rump towards the King, but he had taken such pains to dress it to that duty, that it entered backwards; and at his retreat the spectators clapped." The Deputy Earl Marshal, Lord Effingham, at the same Coronation, was even more unfortunate for he mislaid the Sword of State and forgot to provide the Canopy and the State Banquet Chairs for the King and Queen. He excused himself, however, by owning that "the Earl Marshal's office had been strangely neglected; but he had taken such care for the future, that the *next Coronation* would be regulated in the most exact manner imaginable"—a remark which considerably amused King George III.

In a ceremony exciting such interest as a Coronation incidents such as these are bound to be discussed and recorded in contemporary letters and journals. More curious to modern ideas are the incidents which are recorded as taking place at 18th- and 19th-century Coronations within the Abbey itself, without apparently any suggestion to those who recorded them that they were either incongruous or unseemly. It marks the period when Coronations were regarded as mere shows with little religious significance, and when it was the usual practice for the dean and prebendaries of Westminster to sell the seats in the Nave and elsewhere to the highest bidders. As Horace Walpole remarked, "The prebends would like a coronation every year." Hickey records that when that "dignified and accomplished" prelate, the Archbishop-designate of York (Drummond), mounted the pulpit to preach the sermon at the Coronation of George III, most of the congregation "took that opportunity to eat their meal, when the general clattering of knives, forks, plates, and glasses that ensued, produced a most ridiculous effect, and a universal burst of laughter followed." Again at the Coronation of William IV, when the medals were thrown about during the Homage (a practice discontinued after Queen Victoria's Coronation), a spectator recorded that "it was a fine sight to see all the Judges scrambling for medals, they appeared like so many rams in a pen, butting to get out of it" and this "set the House of Commons in a roar, clapping, etc. Nothing could have been more ludicrous."

In the early part of the 18th century when many were Jacobite at heart, it was, perhaps, understandable for Lady Dorchester (Catherine Sedley), at George I's Coronation, to turn to her neighbour when the Archbishop at the Recognition was asking the consent of the people, and say "Does the old fool think that anybody here will say No when there are so many drawn swords?" There could be no

Charles II is seated crowned on his Throne in the centre of the Theatre. Apart from depicting the Restoration Coronation this contemporary print is of considerable interest as it accurately shows the interior of Westminster Abbey, with its tapestry hangings, High Altar, pulpit, etc., as it was at that date—1661.

James II and Mary of Modena are seen below at their Coronation in 1685 seated on their Thrones with their Supporting Bishops and the four Sword Bearers. Lord Thomas Howard (Lord of the Manor of Worksop) and the Earl of Lindsey (Lord Great Chamberlain) stand on the right and left of the King. The Dean of Westminster (Dr. Sprat) stands on the steps of the Throne and Lord Godolphin (The Queen's Lord Chamberlain) beyond the Queen and her Ladies. All these appear to be careful likenesses. Reproduced from a contemporary engraving by Sandford.

excuse, however, for the fact that "the Duke of Wellington, Lord Grey, Lord Lyndhurst, Lord Hill, but above all Brougham, were loudly cheered" by their respective political parties at the Reform Bill Coronation of William IV. Indeed, as Brougham approached the Throne the members rose, we are told, "*en masse* waving hats, handkerchiefs, and programmes," which, not surprisingly, Macaulay "thought indecorous in such a place and on such an occasion." Such ebullitions were, however, taken for the most part as a matter of course. At the next Coronation in 1838 Marshal Soult was surprised and gratified at the ovation he received, and cheers greater or less greeted the appearance of the Duke of Wellington, Prince Esterhazy ("covered with diamonds and pearls, and as he dangled his hat it cast a dancing radiance all round"), and Lord Melbourne, who was described rather unkindly by the young Disraeli as looking "very awkward and uncouth, with his coronet over his nose, his robes under his feet, and holding the great sword of state like a butcher."

Nor was the demeanour of either George IV or William IV calculated to add to the solemnity of their Coronations. Dignity and a sense of what was fitting were never conspicuous in William IV. He was described as "very awkward," and he considerably disconcerted the Archbishop by presenting himself when disrobed for the Anointing in full Admiral's uniform. George IV, indeed, to the romantic eyes of Sir Walter Scott, looked "every inch a king," but a Westminster boy, writing to his brother, remarked with the distressing candour of youth that when the King entered the Abbey "he looked too large for effect, indeed he was more like an Elephant than a man and there were 10 or 12 persons continually with him to bear up his train." The King was in fact almost overcome with the heat and the weight of his robes throughout the Ceremony. The same Westminster boy learnt from one of his schoolfellows, whose duty it was as one of the Royal Pages to supply the King with pocket handkerchiefs, that no fewer than nineteen were required to mop the Royal brow during the Homage alone, and that "when the Archbishop preached about the burthens of Royalty, the King was observed to wink at the Duke of York and point to his immense train."

The inauspicious beginning of that day of pompous pageantry is well known; how the much-injured Queen Caroline appeared shortly after six o'clock in the morning and made an ill-advised attempt to force her way into the Abbey. She went from door to door only to be told that no place had been provided for her, until at length she was forced to retire discomforted. The close of the day is perhaps less known although it was no less inauspicious. The King was so unpopular and the attitude of the crowds round Westminster Hall appeared to be so hostile that during the Banquet he had to be told that it would be unsafe for him to return to Carlton House by the ordinary route. It was decided, therefore, to make a wide detour through Tothill Fields and the market gardens which at that time stretched from Westminster in the direction of Chelsea. It happened that one of the Officers of the Escort, Lord de Ros, had been at Westminster School. He was in consequence familiar with all this district, and he volunteered

QUEEN ANNE'S CORONATION

Celia Fiennes, a notable diarist of her day, was present at the Coronation of Queen Anne, and in her *Journeys*, gives a vivid description of the Ceremony. She describes, with a woman's eye, how the Queen was dressed in crimson velvet with a train six yards long, "her robe under was of gold tissue, very rich embroidery of jewels about it, her peticoat the same of gold tissue with gold and silver lace, between rows of diamonds embroidered, her linen fine . . . her head was well dressed with diamonds mixed in the hair which . . . brilled and flamed."

She was conducted to the Altar "which was finely decked with gold tissue carpet and fine linen, on the top all the plate of the Abbey set" and there she was met by the Dean of Westminster and the prebends with the Archbishop who were arrayed "in very rich copes and mitres, black velvet embroidered with gold stars, or else tissue of gold and silver." The copes still exist and will be worn at the Coronation of Queen Elizabeth II.

At the Recognition Miss Fiennes saw the Queen "turn her face to the four sides of the Church," and she describes the Anointing and Investing of the Queen. "Then last of all the Archbishops held the Crown over her head, which Crown was made on purpose for this ceremony vastly rich in diamonds, the borders, and the globe part very thick set with vast diamonds, the cross on the top with all diamonds which flamed at the least motion."

The portrait of Queen Anne is by J. Closterman and is now in the National Portrait Gallery.

ENTRY OF THE KING'S CHAMPION

Sandford's fine engraving of the entry of the King's Champion at the Coronation Banquet of James II illustrates this ancient and picturesque custom. The challenge made on this occasion reads as follows:

"If any person, of what degree soever, high or low, shall deny or gainsay our sovereign lord King James the Second, King of England, Scotland, France and Ireland, Defender of the Faith, etc., brother and next heir to our sovereign lord King Charles the Second, the last King deceased, to be right heir to the imperial crown of this realm of Great Britain and Ireland, or that he ought to enjoy the same; here is his Champion, who saith that he lieth, and is a false traitor, being ready in person to combat with him; and in this quarrel will adventure his life against him, on what day soever he shall be appointed."

to pilot the Royal carriages although most of the roads were little better than cart-tracks. All went well, however, until they came "to a broad deep canal, full of water and mud, over which lay an old wooden bridge, stopped up at its entrance by strong barricadoes." It was impossible to turn back and it was decided to risk it. The barricades were knocked down, and first the King's carriage and then all the other carriages got safely over although "the planks cracked, shook, bent, and were all in great holes." Afterwards it was found that the bridge had been condemned for many years as impassably dangerous even for foot passengers. The King, not unnaturally, throughout the drive "was horribly nervous, and kept continually calling to the officers of the escort to keep well up to the carriage windows" as they proceeded through the "Five Fields" (now Eaton Square) and so eventually to the back entrance of Carlton House. They had left Westminster Hall about half-past eight and darkness had long fallen before they finally reached their destination.

It was customary for the King's Herb Woman and her maids to lead the grand procession from Westminster Hall to the Abbey, carpeting the raised platform with fragrant flowers. The office of Herb Woman was much coveted and its origins are probably rooted in the belief that the aroma of sweet herbs was an antidote to plague. The last Herb Woman to perform her pleasant duty was Miss Fellowes. Escorted by Mr. Fellowes (presumably her father) she and her maids elegantly dressed in white strewed flowers in the path of George IV. We are told that as an additional adornment she wore a scarlet mantle tastefully and appropriately decorated with flowers. This reproduction is from a water-colour sketch made of that occasion.

Stating, The Amount, under the several Heads, expended; and from what Sources the Money was supplied.

	£.	s.	d.
Lord Steward, - - - Expenses attending the Banquet - - - - -	25,184	9	8
Lord Chamberlain, - - - for the Furniture and Decorations of Westminster Abbey, and Westminster Hall; for providing the Regalia; for Dresses &c. of the Persons attending and performing various Duties - - - -	111,172	9	10
Master of the Horse, - - - for the Charger for the Champion - -	118	18	6
Master of the Robes, - - - for His Majesty's Robes, &c. - - - -	24,704	8	10
Surveyor General of Works, - - - for fitting up Westminster Abbey, and Westminster Hall, Platforms, &c. - - - - - - - -	50,367	9	1
W. D. Fellowes, Esq. Secretary to His Majesty's Great Chamberlain, - - - for Expenses incurred - - - - - - - -	2,500	—	—
Hire of the Theatres - - - - - - - - -	3,504	15	—
Master of the Mint, - - - for Medals - - - - - - -	4,770	5	4
Sir Geo. Naylor, - - - for Expenses in the Earl Marshal's Department - -	2,500	—	—
Sir Geo. Naylor, - - - towards the Publication of the Account of the Ceremony - - - - - - - - - -	3,000	—	—
Deputy Earl Marshal, - - - usual Fee - - - - -	800	—	—
Sir R. Baker, - - - Expense of Police - - - - - -	981	18	10
Sir T. Tyrwhitt, - - - for Messengers and Door-keepers House of Lords -	173	2	6
Messrs. Rundell and Bridge, - - - for Snuff Boxes for Foreign Ministers -	8,205	15	—
Earl of Kinnoul, - - - on Account of Pursuivants and Heralds in Scotland -	254	7	7
£.	238,238	—	2

Note:— A few Claims are still unsettled, the amount probably not exceeding - - £. 1,000.

	£.	s.	d.
PAID - - - out of the Sum voted by Parliament, in the Session 1820 - -	100,000	—	—
PAID - - - out of Money received from France on Account of pecuniary Indemnity, under Treaty, Anno 1815 - - - - -	138,238	—	2
£.	238,238	—	2

Whitehall, Treasury Chambers,
27th May 1823.

J. C. HERRIES.

GEORGE IV'S LAVISH CROWNING

George IV was crowned amid a display of extravagance of which only he and his time could be capable. The Banquet in Westminster Hall was Lucullian in conception at which the King's Champion accompanied by the Duke of Wellington and the Earl Marshal, all superbly mounted, performed his duty for the last time. The Regalia was reset at a great cost and the Jewelled Sword made specially for the Ceremony. It was a fine day and at first the people were in good humour despite the King's unpopularity. Mrs. Arbuthnot in her *Journal* tells us that: "the nobles and the sages decked out in velvet and satin, gold and jewellery, passed in procession through countless thousands . . . all uniting to do homage to the Constitution." Later in the day there was to be some hostility from the crowds. The King, sixty years old and obese, was bowed down by the weight of his robes and jewels. He wore a wig with curls that hung down his back, and as he had only recently recovered from an operation he was a little pale and weak. Nevertheless, he was able to stand the strain of the long and arduous ceremonies though at times he did seem to be a little impatient. Two years later the account was presented. The cost was enormous. The balance sheet of one of the most lavish Coronations ever staged is reproduced above.

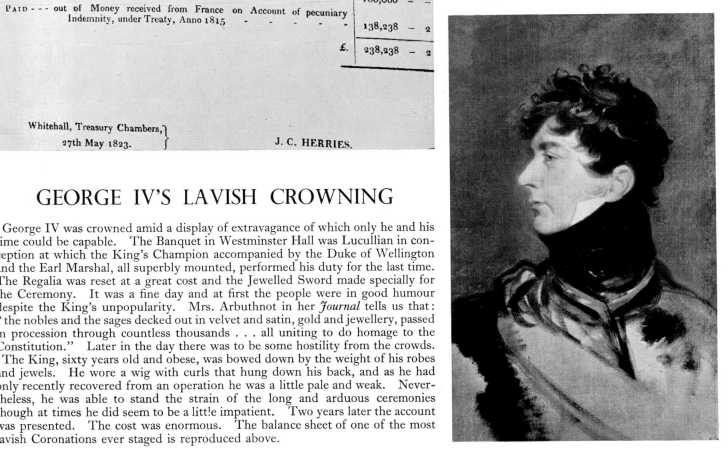

King's Coronation 1821

CENTRAL PAVILION,
PALACE YARD.

Refreshments,

FURNISHED BY MESS^{RS}. WAUD AND PERRY,

AT THE FOLLOWING PRICES.

	£.	s.	d.		£.	s.	d.
Chicken	0	4	0	Coffee	0	1	0
Lobster	0	3	0	Lemonade	0	1	0
Lamb	0	5	0	Ice	0	1	0
Ham	0	2	0	Negus	0	1	0
Beef	0	1	6	Jelly	0	1	0
Salad	0	1	0	Soda Water	0	1	0
Sandwich	0	1	0	Ginger Beer	0	1	0
Porter	0	0	6	Strawberries	0	1	0
Roll	0	0	2	Oranges	0	1	0
Savoy Cake	0	2	6	Port Wine, or }	0	7	0
Tart	0	2	0	Sherry }			
Tea	0	1	0	Cyder	0	2	0

Biscuits, Cakes, &c. proportionably cheap.

GLINDON, Printer, Rupert Street.

This price list of refreshments available in a stand from which George IV's procession from Westminster Hall to the Abbey could be viewed provides a gastronomic sidelight on the period. Lamb, it would seem, was the most expensive meat, whilst lobster was less of a luxury than chicken. Beverages were all expensive but no doubt Messrs. Waud and Perry's prices were suitably inflated for the expensive occasion.

*   *   *

The portrait below of George IV by Sir Thomas Lawrence, R.A., is reproduced by permission of the National Portrait Gallery.

The Coronation of George IV. The Archbishop places the Crown on the King's head. The Dean of Westminster stands facing the King, behind him is the Lord Chancellor and the Duke of Wellington. The Duke of York stands next to the bishops.

In the reproduction below, appearing, as Arthur Bryant has written in *The Age of Elegance*, as "a gorgeous bird of the East," George IV with his train-bearers advances along the flower-strewn platform which led from Westminster Hall to the Abbey.

The scene depicted above is the entry of the first course at the Coronation Banquet of George IV in Westminster Hall in 1821. The Marquess of Anglesey, Lord High Steward, on his favourite dun-coloured Arabian, is in the centre. On his right is the Duke of Wellington, the Lord High Constable, and on his left is Lord Howard of Effingham, the Deputy Earl Marshal.

A reproduction, below, of the Procession of the Regalia in Westminster Hall at the same Coronation shows the Dean of Westminster, bearing St. Edward's Crown, approaching the King, who is seated under a canopy, surrounded by the Great Officers of State. Behind the dean follow the prebendaries of Westminster bearing the rest of the Regalia.

King George V and Queen Mary seated upon their Chairs of Estate before the Service began.

THE CORONATION OF KING GEORGE V

" *Thursday, June 22nd* [1911]. *Our Coronation Day. Buckingham Palace.* It was overcast & cloudy with some showers & a strongish cool breeze, but better for the people than great heat. Today was indeed a great & memorable day in our lives & one we can never forget, but it brought back to me many sad memories of 9 years ago, when the beloved Parents were crowned. May & I left B.P. in the Coronation coach at 10.30 with 8 cream-coloured horses. There were over 50,000 troops lining the streets under the command of Lord Kitchener. There were hundreds of thousands of people who gave us a magnificent reception. The Service in the Abbey was most beautiful, but it was a terrible ordeal. It was grand, yet simple & most dignified and went without a hitch. I nearly broke down when dear David came to do homage to me, as it reminded me so much when I did the same thing to beloved Papa, he did it so well. Darling May looked lovely & it was indeed a comfort to me to have her by my side, as she has been ever to me during these last eighteen years.

We left Westminster Abbey at 2.15 (having arrived there before 11.0) with our Crowns on and sceptres in our hands. This time we drove by the Mall, St. James' Street & Piccadilly, crowds enormous & decorations very pretty. On reaching B.P. just before 3.0 May & I went out on the balcony to show ourselves to the people. Downey photographed us in our robes with Crowns on. Had some lunch with our guests here. Worked all the afternoon with Bigge & others answering telegrams & letters of which I have had hundreds. Such a large crowd collected in front of the Palace that I went out on the balcony again. Our guests dined with us at 8.30. May & I showed ourselves again to the people. Wrote & read. Rather tired. Bed at 11.45. Beautiful illuminations everywhere."

This extract from the King's diary now in the Royal Archives at Windsor was first published by gracious permission of Her Majesty the Queen in *King George V, His Life and Reign* by Harold Nicolson (Constable, *42s.* net).

The photograph above and that on the facing page are historic since they were the first ever taken at an English Coronation. The photographer was Sir Benjamin Stone, Royal Photographer to King George V, who exposed a number of negatives from a hidden view-point opposite the Royal Gallery. The first photo-graph shows King George V and Queen Mary seated in their Chairs of Estate before the Service began; in the second the ritual of the Recognition is about to commence. Both are repro-duced by permission from the Sir Benjamin Stone Collection of photographs in Birmingham Reference Library.

The Crowning of Queen Victoria, 28th June, 1838.   An engraving from the painting made in the Abbey by Arthur Newcombe, R.A.

7

CORONATIONS OF QUEENS REGNANT

UEEN ELIZABETH II is the sixth Queen Regnant of England. Her predecessors were Mary I (1553–58), Elizabeth I (1558–1603), Mary II (1689–94), Anne (1702–14) and Victoria (1837–1901). Two others, indeed, might claim a like title, but neither the Empress Matilda, the daughter of Henry I, although she assumed the title of "Domina" during the few months in 1141 in which she deposed her cousin Stephen, nor the ill-fated Lady Jane Grey, who ruled for nine days, were ever crowned.

The first Coronation of a Queen Regnant was that of Queen Mary I on 1st October, 1553. The times were difficult, but the customary progress from the Tower to Whitehall with the usual pageantry was carried out without mishap, and the next day the Queen proceeded by barge from Whitehall to Westminster Hall and thence to the Abbey. The Archbishops of Canterbury (Cranmer) and York (Holgate) and the Bishop of London (Ridley) were prisoners in the Tower for "treason or great crimes." It fell, therefore, to the Bishop of Winchester (Gardiner) to officiate at the Coronation, and the sermon was preached by Bishop Day of Chichester, "the floridest preacher" of the time. The Queen had doubts whether the holy oil, which had been used since the reign of Henry IV, might not have lost its efficacy, and, in consequence, a fresh supply, blessed by the Bishop of Arras, was procured from overseas.

It is said, too, that the Queen disliked the idea of being crowned in King Edward's Chair, on the ground that it had been used by her Protestant brother, Edward VI, and therefore a chair which had been blessed by the Pope was provided instead. If this is so it may well be the chair, now in Winchester Cathedral, which was almost certainly used at the Queen's subsequent marriage to Philip of Spain. There may, indeed, be some truth in the tradition as far as the Coronation is concerned, for although the chair in which the Queen was crowned is merely described as "a rich chair before the high altar," it is a remarkable fact that King Edward's Chair, probably for the only time in its history, was used as the Throne for the Homage. We are told that after the Queen had been crowned with three crowns—King Edward's, the Imperial Crown, and "a very rich crown, purposely made for her Grace"—she was "conveyed" to King Edward's Chair on "the

73

mount" (*i.e.* the Theatre). It is described as "a great royal chair . . . having pillars at the back, whereon stood two lions of gold, and in the midst a turret with a flower de lice of gold." The lions and the fleur-de-lys have disappeared, but the places where they were fixed still remain. At the Banquet after the Ceremony the Queen's stepmother, Anne of Cleves, who had emerged from her seclusion in order to be present at the Service in the Abbey, and the Queen's sister, the Lady Elizabeth, both sat at the Royal table.

Elizabeth's own Coronation was to follow six years later. The progress from the Tower has been pictured in a contemporary MS. now at the British Museum, part of which may be seen on page 55. It shows the Queen being drawn along in an open chariot accompanied by a brilliant cavalcade. Elizabeth, who prided herself on her scholarship and powers of repartee, won golden opinions by her gracious demeanour and by the ease and skill with which she replied to the greetings in Latin and English which were presented to her by allegorical figures who met her at every stage of the progress.

The Service in the Abbey was the last which was performed in conformity with Roman Catholic usage. There were, however, some significant innovations. Although the greater part of the Service was in Latin, the Litany was read in English and the Epistle and Gospel were read first in Latin and then in English. Moreover it would appear that during the celebration of the Mass Elizabeth deliberately withdrew into her Traverse behind the High Altar in order to avoid being present at the consecration and elevation of the Host. From religious scruples many of the bishops refused to be present in the Abbey, and the whole Ceremony was conducted by Bishop Oglethorpe of Carlisle to whom the Queen remarked that "the oil was grease and smelt ill." The Service was in fact a compromise and there must have been a sense of strain throughout. Small wonder that when the Service in the Abbey was successfully completed the Queen "returned very cheerfully, with a most smiling countenance for everyone, giving them all a thousand greetings," although the eye-witness adds disapprovingly that by so doing in his opinion "she exceeded the bounds of gravity and decorum."

Over a hundred years was to elapse before the Coronation of the next Queen Regnant in 1689. The occasion was unusual inasmuch as King William and Queen Mary had been declared King and Queen of England for their joint and separate lives. At their Coronation, therefore, they proceeded up the Abbey not as King and Consort but side by side with the Sword of State and their Regalia borne in front of them. A special chair had been made for the Queen closely resembling the historic chair of King Edward. These two chairs were placed in front of the Thrones and facing the Altar, and in them the King and Queen, one immediately after the other, were anointed and invested with the Royal robes and insignia. Only the King, however, was actually girt with the Sword. By a curious mistake the Coronation rings got mixed, and the Queen's ruby Ring, which had been given to her on her marriage and which she had had enlarged for the Coronation, was placed in error on the King's finger. Finally,

This portrait of Queen Elizabeth I is of the English School, *circa* 1588. The panels, left and right, of ships in a calm sea and in a tempest are believed to depict the defeat of the Spanish Armada in 1588, which the artist probably intended to commemorate. The painting is in the Woburn Abbey Collection and is reproduced by kind permission of The Duke of Bedford.

THE CORONATION OF THE FIRST QUEEN ELIZABETH

Although only one contemporary illustration of the Coronation of Queen Elizabeth I is known to exist (see page 55), fairly full accounts of the occasion were recorded, particularly by Holinshed in his *Chronicles* published in 1587. There was the progress from the Tower to Westminster. During this, according to a pamphlet entitled *The Passage of our most drad Soveraigne Lady Quene Elyzabeth the daye before her coronacion* published in London by R. Tothill, 1559, a poor woman made the Queen a gift of rosemary, and a child presented Her Majesty with a Bible after prettily reciting some verses interpretating the Pageant of Truth. "When the childe had thus ended his speache, he reached his booke towardes the Quenes maiestie, which a little before Trueth had let downe unto him from the hill, whiche by sir John Parrat was received and delivered unto the Quene. But she as soone as she had receyved the booke kissed it, and with both her handes held up the same, and so laid it upon her brest, with great thankes to the citie therfore."

Holinshed also describes these same charming incidents and then continues: "On Sundaie the five and twentieth of Januarie [1559], hir maiestie was with great solemnitie crowned at Westminster in the abbeie church there, by doctor Oglethorpe bishop of Carleill. She dined in Westminster hall, which was richlie hung, and everie thing ordered in such roiall maner, as to such a regall and most solemne feast apperteined. In the meanetime, whilest hir grace sat at dinner sir Edward Dimmocke knight, hir champion by office, came riding into the hall in faire complet armor, mounted upon a beautifull courser, richlie trapped in cloth of gold, entred the hall, and in the midst thereof cast downe his gantlet: with offer to fight with him in hir quarell, that should denie hir to be the righteous and lawfull queene of this realme. The queene taking a cup of gold full of wine, dranke to him thereof, and sent it to him for his fee together with the cover."

The introduction of English into parts of the Service at this Coronation—the last performed in conformity with the usages of the Roman Church—incensed all the Marian bishops to such an extent that they absented themselves with the exception of Owen Oglethorpe, Bishop of Carlisle, who conducted the Service and crowned the Queen. Her Majesty appeared to be pleased with the arrangements but she complained sharply about the smell of the Oil. Bishop Oglethorpe's loyalty to Elizabeth availed him little for in the same year he was deprived.

still seated side by side, they were crowned in turn and proceeded together to their Thrones where they received the Homage of their subjects. The Service had started late and darkness had fallen before the Banquet was concluded in Westminster Hall. Even in the Abbey the Princess Anne "observing that her Majesty seem'd a little discomposed with the variety of the Ceremonies, and the Burthen of the Regalia," had whispered to her "Madam, I pity your fatigue." The remark was not well received, for the Queen, who was not on the best of terms with her sister, snapped back, "A crown, sister, is not so heavy as it seems."

Anne's own Coronation was remarkable for the fact that for the first time a Queen Regnant was accompanied by a husband who was not himself a Sovereign. Elizabeth I was unmarried, Mary I and, in later days, Victoria were married after their Coronations had taken place, and Mary II shared the Sovereignty with her husband. Unfortunately, for future ages, Prince George of Denmark made so little impression on his contemporaries that no one seems to have remembered to record exactly what he did or where he sat during the actual Service. It is known, however, that he took his place in the Procession immediately in front of those carrying the Regalia, and that, somewhat unexpectedly, he did Homage as Duke of Cumberland first of all and before the archbishops and bishops. It will be interesting to see how far these precedents are followed at the forthcoming Coronation. The Queen herself was crippled with gout and got through the Service with some difficulty, having "for conveniency to be carried in a low open chair" by four Yeoman of the Guard in the Procession.

No such infirmity marked the Coronation of Queen Victoria. The young Queen might be little known to her subjects, but the contrast between her radiant health and vitality and the decrepitude of her immediate predecessors caused a great outburst of popular enthusiasm and loyalty.

The Service itself was interminably long—it lasted five hours—and suffered all too obviously from lack of rehearsal. No one except the Queen, the archbishop, and Lord John Thynne, who as sub-dean was acting for the Dean of Westminster, seemed to have the least idea what was happening or what was to be done next and the result was "continual difficulty and embarrassment." The bishops started the Litany before the delivery of the Regalia and as they could not be stopped both proceeded together. Later the Service was momentarily suspended owing to a discussion as to which finger the Ring was to be put upon. The archbishop eventually insisted on following the rubric and forced it on to the fourth finger, causing the Queen considerable pain as, by mistake, it had been made to fit her little finger.

None-the-less the Service made a great impression on those who were present, and it was redeemed throughout by the dignity and self-possession of the young and diminutive Queen. There was, for instance, the incident during the Homage when old Lord Rolle tripped as he mounted the steps of the Throne. After a moment's consternation the Queen whispered to Lord Melbourne, and then rose and advanced to meet Lord Rolle, who was making repeated efforts to

CORONATION SOUVENIRS

To commemorate Queen Victoria's Coronation, souvenirs of many kinds were made and sold in hundreds of thousands. Mugs, effigies, china plaques, medals and portraits were especially popular. One souvenir— now a collector's piece—more ingenious and expensive than most was "*Fores' Correct Representation of the State Procession of Her Majesty's Coronation.*" It consists of two paper strips each thirty feet long on which are lithographed the entire Coronation Procession in correct order and minute detail. The two strips fold concertina fashion between book covers which are fastened with a brass clasp. The photograph (*left*), gives a general impression of the souvenir, which cost £1 11s. 6d. coloured and 16s. plain, and below three short sections of the beautifully drawn "strip" are reproduced.

The Band of the Household Brigade.

The Carriage of the Queen's Ladies.

The Queen's Escort of Life Guards.

remount the steps, extending her hand and bowing her head so that he could touch the Crown without further exertion. No one who saw the incident ever forgot the consummate grace and charm of the Queen's action.

Then there was the muddle that occurred towards the close of the Service. A pencil note made by Lord John Thynne in his copy of the Order of the Service states that after the *Gloria in Excelsis* "the Bishop of Bath and Wells (supposed from turning over two pages) informed H.M. that the Service was concluded and H.M. retired to the Confessor's Chapel. The Sub Dean inquired of the Ld. Chamberlain (Conyngham) if H.M. was ill. 'No,' said he, 'all is over.' Being told that it was not all over reference was made to H.M. & by her order to the Sub Dean for advice. He referred the L.Ch. to the Prime Minister (Melbourne) who replied 'What does it signify.' H.M. again sent to the Sub Dean for advice and he advised H.M. to return to her Chair under and by the throne." The Queen, therefore, returned leaning on Lord Melbourne's arm, and the Service concluded. But even then the confusion was not at an end. In St. Edward's Chapel, before the final Procession started for the West Door, "the Archbishop came in" as the Queen herself recorded in her *Journal*, "and *ought* to have delivered the Orb to me, but I had already got it, and he (as usual) was *so* confused and puzzled and knew nothing, and went away."

The Orb of England (*left*), placed only in the hand of the Sovereign, and the Queen Consort's Orb.

The painting by Sir George Hayter, portrait and historical painter to Queen Victoria.

THE CROWNING OF QUEEN VICTORIA

The Coronation of Queen Victoria was an event of immense popular interest and genuine rejoicing. The young and intelligent Queen Regnant had been accepted with acclaim, and as her Coronation Day approached the public fervour rose to a crescendo.

Only seven years earlier London had witnessed the austerity crowning of her uncle, William IV. Then the Abbey Service had been curtailed, the Banquet in Westminster Hall abandoned and the ceremonies shorn of much of the traditional splendour and pageantry. For the Coronation of the nineteen-year-old Queen, the Service was enacted with all its ancient ritual, and afterwards there was a triumphant progress and illuminations and entertainments for the people. Although the Banquet was not held, there was a family dinner party at Buckingham Palace; yet despite the strain and exertions of the day, the Queen that night was able to write in her *Journal* a detailed and vivid account of her crowning. It makes fascinating reading and the following long extract from it is a fitting accompaniment to the illustrations of a truly historic occasion.

Thursday, 28th June, 1838.

I was awoke at four o'clock by the guns in the Park, and could not get much sleep afterwards on account of the noise of the people, bands, etc., etc. Got up at seven, feeling strong and well; the Park presented a curious spectacle, crowds of people up to Constitution Hill, soldiers, bands, etc. I dressed, having taken a little breakfast before I dressed, and a little after. At half-past 9 I went into the next room, dressed exactly in my House of Lords costume; and met Uncle Ernest, Charles,[1] and Feodore (who had come a few minutes before into my dressing-room), Lady Lansdowne, Lady Normanby, the Duchess of Sutherland, and Lady Barham, all in their robes.

At 10 I got into the State Coach with the Duchess of Sutherland and Lord Albemarle and we began our Progress. I subjoin a minute account of the whole Procession and of the whole Proceeding,—the route, etc. It was a fine day, and the crowds of people exceeded what I have ever seen; many as there were the day I went to the City, it was nothing, nothing to the multitudes, the millions of my loyal subjects, who were assembled *in every spot* to witness the Procession. Their good humour and excessive loyalty was beyond everything, and I really cannot say *how* proud I feel to be the Queen of *such* a Nation. I was alarmed at times for fear that the people would be crushed and squeezed on account of the tremendous rush and pressure.

I reached the Abbey amid deafening cheers at a little after half-past eleven; I first went into a robing-room quite close to the entrance where I found my eight train-bearers: Lady Caroline

[1] Prince Charles of Leiningen, the Queen's half-brother.

The portrait at Windsor Castle by Sir George Hayter.

The Crowning of Queen Victoria (cont.)

Lennox, Lady Adelaide Paget, Lady Mary Talbot, Lady Fanny Cowper, Lady Wilhelmina Stanhope, Lady Anne Fitzwilliam, Lady Mary Grimston, and Lady Louisa Jenkinson—all dressed alike and beautifully in white satin and silver tissue with wreaths of silver corn-ears in front, and a small one of pink roses round the plait behind, and pink roses in the trimming of the dresses.

After putting on my mantle, and the young ladies having properly got hold of it and Lord Conyngham holding the end of it, I left the robing-room and the Procession began. . . .

The sight was splendid; the bank of Peeresses quite beautiful all in their robes, and the Peers on the other side. My young train-bearers were always near me, and helped me whenever I wanted anything. The Bishop of Durham stood on the side near me, but he was, as Lord Melbourne told me, remarkably *maladroit*, and never could tell me what was to take place. At the beginning of the Anthem, where I've made a mark, I retired to St. Edward's Chapel, a dark small place immediately behind the Altar, with my ladies and train-bearers—took off my crimson robe and kirtle, and put on the supertunica of cloth of gold, also in the shape of a kirtle, which was put over a singular sort of little gown of linen trimmed with lace; I also took off my circlet of diamonds and then proceeded bareheaded into the Abbey; I was then seated upon St. Edward's chair, where the Dalmatic robe was clasped round me by the Lord Great Chamberlain. Then followed all the various things; and last (of those things) the Crown being placed on my head—which was, I must own, a most beautiful impressive moment; *all* the Peers and Peeresses put on their coronets at the same instant.

My excellent Lord Melbourne, who stood very close to me throughout the whole ceremony, was *completely* overcome at this moment, and very much affected; he gave me *such* a kind, and I may say *fatherly* look. The shouts, which were very great, the drums, the trumpets, the firing of the guns, all at the same instant, rendered the spectacle most imposing.

The Enthronisation and the Homage of, first, all the Bishops, and then my Uncles, and lastly of all the Peers, in their respective order was very fine. The Duke of Norfolk (holding for me the Sceptre with a Cross) with Lord Melbourne stood close to me on my right, and the Duke of Richmond with the other Sceptre on my left, etc., etc. All my train-bearers, etc., standing behind the Throne. Poor old Lord Rolle, who is 82, and dreadfully infirm, in attempting to ascend the steps fell and rolled quite down, but was not the least hurt; when he attempted to re-ascend them I got up and advanced to the end of the steps, in order to prevent another fall. When Lord Melbourne's turn to do Homage came, there was loud cheering; they also cheered Lord Grey and the Duke of Wellington; it's a pretty ceremony; they first all touch the Crown, and then kiss my hand. When my good Lord Melbourne knelt down and kissed my hand, he pressed my hand and I grasped his with all my heart, at which he looked up with his eyes filled with tears and seemed much touched, as he was, I observed, throughout the whole ceremony. After the Homage was concluded I left the Throne, took off my Crown and received the Sacrament; I then put on my Crown again, and re-ascended the Throne, leaning on Lord Melbourne's arm. At the commencement of the Anthem I descended from the Throne, and went into St. Edward's Chapel with my Ladies, Train-bearers, and Lord Willoughby, where I took off the Dalmatic robe, supertunica, etc., and put on the Purple Velvet Kirtle and Mantle, and proceeded again to the Throne, which I ascended leaning on Lord Melbourne's hand.

I then again descended from the Throne, and repaired with all the Peers bearing the Regalia, my Ladies and Train-bearers, to St. Edward's Chapel, as it is called; but which, as Lord Melbourne said, was more *un*like a Chapel than anything he had ever seen; for what was *called* an *Altar* was covered with sandwiches, bottles of wine, etc., etc. The Archbishop came in and *ought* to have delivered the Orb to me, but I had already got it, and he (as usual) was *so* confused and puzzled and knew nothing, and—went away. Here we waited some minutes. Lord Melbourne took a glass of wine, for he seemed completely tired. The Procession being formed, I replaced my Crown (which I had taken off for a few minutes), took the Orb in my left hand and the Sceptre in my right, and thus *loaded*, proceeded through the Abbey—which resounded with cheers, to the first robing-room; where I found the Duchess of Gloucester, Mamma, and the Duchess of Cambridge with their Ladies. . . . The Archbishop had (most awkwardly) put the ring on the wrong finger, and the consequence was that I had the greatest difficulty to take it off again, which I at last did with great pain. At about half-past four I re-entered my carriage, the Crown on my head, and the Sceptre and Orb in my hands, and we proceeded the same way as we came—the crowds if possible having increased. The enthusiasm, affection, and loyalty were really touching, and I shall ever remember this day as the *Proudest* of my life! I came home at a little after six, really *not* feeling tired.

At eight we dined. Besides we thirteen—my Uncles, sister, brother, Späth, and the Duke's gentlemen—my excellent Lord Melbourne and Lord Surrey dined here. Lord Melbourne came up to me and said: "I must congratulate you on this most brilliant day," and that all had gone off so well. He said he was not tired, and was in high spirits. I sat between Uncle Ernest [1] and Lord Melbourne; and Lord Melbourne between me and Feodore, whom he had led in. My kind Lord Melbourne was much affected in speaking of the whole ceremony. He asked kindly if I was tired; said the Sword he carried (the first, the

[1] The King of Hanover.

Queen Victoria taking the Sacrament at her Coronation.   After Charles Robert Leslie.

The Crowning of Queen Victoria (cont.)

Sword of State) was excessively heavy.   I said that the Crown hurt me a good deal.   He was so much amused at Uncle Ernest's being astonished at our still having the Litany.   We agreed that the whole thing was a very fine sight.   He thought the robes, and particularly the Dalmatic, "looked remarkably well."   "And you did it all so well—excellent!" said he, with tears in his eyes. He said he thought I looked rather pale and "moved by all the people" when I arrived; "and that's natural; and that's better." The Archbishop's and Dean's copes, which were remarkably handsome, were from James the Second's time; the very same that were worn at his Coronation, Lord Melbourne told me. Spoke of the Bishop of Durham's awkwardness, Lord Rolle's fall, etc. . . .

After dinner, before we sat down, we (that is Charles, Lord Melbourne, and I) spoke of the numbers of Peers at the Coronation, which, Lord Melbourne said, with the tears in his eyes, was unprecedented.   I observed that there were very few Viscounts; he said: "There are very few Viscounts," that they were an odd sort of title and not really English; that they came from *Vice-Comités*; that Dukes and Barons were the only *real* English titles; that Marquises were likewise not English; and that they made people Marquises when they did not wish to make them Dukes.   Spoke of Lord Audley who came as the First Baron, and who Lord Melbourne said was a very odd young man.

I said to Lord Melbourne when I first sat down that I felt a little tired on my feet; "You must be very tired," he said. Spoke of the weight of the Robes, etc., etc., the Coronets; and he turned round to me with the tears in his eyes, and said *so* kindly: "And you did it beautifully—every part of it, with so much taste; it's a thing that you can't give a person advice upon; it must be left to a person."   To hear this, from this kind impartial friend, gave me great and real pleasure.   Mamma and Feodore came back just after he said this.   Spoke of the Bishops' Copes, about which he was very funny; of the Pages who were such a nice set of boys, and who were so handy. . . .

He (Lord Melbourne) said there was a large breakfast in the Jerusalem Chamber where they met *before* all began; he said, laughing, that whenever the Clergy, or a Dean and Chapter, had anything to do with anything, there's sure to be plenty to eat.

Spoke of my intending to go to bed, etc.; he said, "You may depend upon it, you are more tired than you think you are."   I said I had slept badly the night before; he said that was my mind, that nothing kept people more awake than any consciousness of a great event going to take place, and being agitated.   He was not sure if he was not going to the Duke of Wellington's.

Stayed in the dining room till twenty minutes past eleven, but remained on Mamma's balcony looking at the fireworks in Green Park, which were quite beautiful.

The Coronation Chair is inseparable from the history of the Coronations of English Kings. The high regard in which it is held is only comparable with the Chair of St. Peter in Rome, and that of St. Augustine in the Cathedral at Canterbury. It is in this Chair that our Kings are anointed, though probably only since the time of Charles I. Likewise it is in this Chair that Sovereigns receive the Royal ornaments, and the Crown. It is the centre of attention at the most significant points of the Coronation Service, during which it stands in the centre of the Theatre facing the High Altar.

8

THE CORONATION CHAIR: THE REGALIA

OR six hundred years the Coronation Chair has been preserved within the Abbey Church of Westminster. It has been used at every Coronation since that of Edward II in 1308. When Edward I captured the Stone of Scone in 1296 he originally intended to enclose it in a bronze chair, but for some reason he changed his mind and decided that it should be made of wood instead. It was, therefore, constructed of oak, at a cost of 100 shillings, and was completed by 1300–1.

The Chair has a high plain back which rises to a crocketed gable originally surmounted by a gold *fleur-de-lys*. The side turrets had little gold lions. The whole Chair was enriched with gilt gesso decoration and glass mosaic. Little now remains of the painted seated figure of a king, the work of Walter of Durham, the King's painter, which decorated the back of the Chair on the inside, but there are panels on the inside faces of the arms of the Chair decorated with naturalistic foliage, birds, and grotesques. The Chair has been shamefully treated in the past, and in the 18th century Westminster boys and others seem to have carved their names at will on the woodwork. Four small lions, which appear to be contemporary, support the Chair, and beneath the seat is a cavity in which rests the Stone of Scone.

The Stone itself is of reddish-grey sandstone. It has an immense legendary history which connects it with the stone upon which Jacob laid his head and dreamed his dream. Actually it would appear to come from the neighbourhood of Scone where rocks of this type are found. Its authenticated history begins with the 13th century. It was then preserved at the Abbey of Scone, where it was used as a seat at the consecration of Scottish Kings. There is, indeed, some slight evidence to suggest that it was originally a stone chair, and that at some period it was reduced to its present rectangular shape.

It should be remembered that the Coronation Chair was made to enclose the Stone, and that together they have acquired a symbolic significance through centuries of historic association with the supreme moment at successive Coronations. Only twice has the Chair left the Abbey. It was taken over to Westminster Hall for the Installation of Oliver Cromwell as Lord Protector, and during the 1939–45 War it was removed for safety to Gloucester Cathedral. The Stone, however, remained within the Abbey, until it was forcibly removed on Christmas Day 1951 and taken to Scotland. After a few weeks it was recovered and has now been replaced under the Chair.

The fact that the Chair was taken over to Westminster Hall for the Installation of Cromwell as Lord Protector in 1657 showed that the tide was beginning to turn in favour of Monarchy. Although he himself refused the title of king, and described the Crown as a "shining bauble for crowds to gaze on," he was ceremonially enthroned in the Chair and invested with a robe of purple velvet lined with ermine, while a sword and a sceptre "of massy gold" were placed in his hands. There is, indeed, some evidence that a crown was actually made for him, and this may be the "imperial crown" which, three years later, was placed by the side of his effigy when it lay in state after his death in Somerset House.

It showed how times had changed. Sixteen years before the notorious Henry Marten, by order of Parliament, had seized the keys of the Treasury at Westminster, and "having forced open a great iron chest, took out the Crowns, the Robes, the Sword and Sceptre, belonging anciently to King Edward the Confessor and used by all our Kings at their Inaugurations." Then, to the disgust of the Sub Dean of Westminster, Peter Heylin, who was present and recorded the fact, he declared that "there would be no further use of those Toys and Trifles," and, "in the jollity of that humour," proceeded to dress up the poet, George Wither, in the robes and put the Crown upon his head. The Regalia, however, appears to have been left at Westminster until 1649, when it was removed to the Tower, where an inventory was made of it and of the other Crown Jewels. The inventory is melancholy reading. All these priceless objects, with their agelong associations, are noted as having been "totallie broken and defaced" and then sent to the Mint to be coined. Heylin, however, recorded that Sir Henry Mildmay, the Keeper of the Jewel House, "first pickt out the richest jewels, and then compounded for the rest at an easie rate." This may partly account for the fact that some of the more famous jewels, such as the Black Prince's Ruby, reappeared at the Restoration. It is even possible that they were bought by Cromwell himself.

But however this may be, the fact remains that most of the Regalia which is used at a modern Coronation was made for the Coronation of Charles II in 1661, by Robert Vyner, the King's Goldsmith, at a total cost of £31,978 9s. 11d. Among the archives of Westminster Abbey is "A memoriall for my honoured friend, Dr. Earles, Dean of Westminster," written by Sir Edward Walker, Garter King of Arms, a few days before that Coronation. It informs the dean that he is to receive "from the Master of the Jewell house by the Lord Chamberlaines warrant these Regalityes which are all new made: St. Edward's staffe, the Scepter with the Crosse, the Scepter with the Dove, the Ampull for the Oyle with a spoone, the Chalice, the Paten, the Crown called St. Edward's which is to be layd ready on the Altar . . . another Crowne and to lay it upon St. Edward's Altar within."

St. Edward's Crown was remade for the Coronation of King Charles II in 1661. It is this Crown which the Dean of Westminster, by traditional right, carries from the High Altar to give to the Archbishop of Canterbury to be by him reverently placed upon the Sovereign's head. The heavily jewelled gold circlet and arched frame now contains the Cap of Estate, but historically the Cap should be worn separately, and the Crown should be a crown pure and simple. The Crown is substantially the same as it was made by Vyner in 1661 after the pattern of the ancient crown of the same name which was destroyed in 1649.

The reference to the Ampulla as among the things "which are all new made" is interesting, for there is a persistent tradition that both it and the Anointing Spoon escaped destruction in 1649. Sandford, indeed, who ought to have known, writing in 1687, when Vyner was alive, definitely states this as a fact. It is possible that Vyner re-fashioned it at a cost of £102 5s. 0d., but, if so, it is difficult to reconcile its present appearance with the descriptions of the medieval Ampulla ("a dove of gold set with pearls and stones") given in the inventory of 1649. The Eagle itself is of gold, nine inches high, and shows no signs of ever having been set with precious stones. It stands on a small pedestal, which is certainly of 17th-century work, with wings outstretched. The head unscrews, and the oil is poured out through the beak. The Spoon is unquestionably the oldest object amongst the Regalia. The bowl may have been remade by Vyner in 1661, but the stem is of early 13th-century date, and may possibly be even older.

St. Edward's Crown, with which the Sovereign is actually crowned, remains substantially as it was made by Vyner. It is a circlet of gold surmounted by alternate *crosses pattée* and *fleur-de-lys* studded with precious stones. From the crosses rise two intersecting gold arches surmounted by a mound and jewelled cross with drop-shaped pearl pendants. The Crown is of considerable weight and is usually exchanged after a few minutes for the Imperial Crown. King George VI, however, wore it for nearly three-quarters of an hour. The Imperial Crown made by Vyner for Charles II is now no longer used. The frame, dismantled of its jewels but with the socket wherein was fixed the Black Prince's Ruby clearly visible, is now on view at the London Museum. The present Imperial Crown was made for Queen Victoria's Coronation by Messrs. Rundell and Bridge in 1838. It is entirely encrusted with precious stones. In front is the Black Prince's Ruby, which was given to him by Pedro the Cruel in 1367, and is said to have been worn by Henry V in his helmet at Agincourt. Immediately below it is the second largest portion of the Star of Africa (Cullinan) diamond ($309\frac{1}{16}$ carats). It was set in this position in 1911 and displaced the Stuart sapphire which is now set in the back of the Crown. This sapphire, which is oval in shape, was among the Crown Jewels of Charles II. It was taken to France by James II, and, after remaining with the exiled House of Stuart, was eventually bequeathed to George III by Henry, Cardinal York. In the centre of the *cross pattée* on the top of the Crown is the beautiful sapphire which is believed to have belonged to Edward the Confessor, and at the point of intersection of the arches of the Crown are four large drop-shaped pearls which are traditionally said to have been the ear-rings of Queen Elizabeth I. It is this Crown which is worn at the State Openings of Parliament.

The rest of the Regalia may be described in the order in which it is used in the Service. St. Edward's Staff, nearly five feet long, is tipped with a pike of steel. The staff is of gold and is surmounted by a ball and cross. It is now only carried in the Procession, but originally it seems to have been used by the Sovereign to walk with in the procession from Westminster Hall to the Abbey in the same way

The Imperial State Crown consists of a circlet of silver open-work, bordered with pearls and set with clusters of emeralds, sapphires, and diamonds. Above this circlet are four *fleur-de-lys* and four *crosses pattée*, as in St. Edward's Crown, but entirely set with diamonds and gems. The arches of the Crown are worked into a design of oak leaves and acorns. The diamond mound is surmounted by a diamond *cross pattée* with a sapphire in the centre of the cross. Some of the historic gems set in this Crown are discussed in the text. In the illustration can be seen the Black Prince's Ruby, with part of the Star of Africa diamond set in the circlet beneath it. From the arches depend four pearls traditionally believed to have been Queen Elizabeth I's ear-rings, and, above all, set in the uppermost cross is the beautiful sapphire which is said to have belonged to St. Edward.

that a bishop carries a crozier. It dates from 1661, as do also the gold "prick" Spurs, although buckles have been subsequently added to them.

From the earliest days ceremonial swords have been carried before Sovereigns at their Coronations. Five such swords are used at a modern Coronation. The most imposing is the great two-handed Sword of State in its rich scabbard of crimson velvet embellished with Royal badges. This is carried not only at a Coronation but also at the State Openings of Parliament. The personal sword of the Sovereign—known as the Jewelled Sword—which is offered at the Altar during the Service, was made for the Coronation of George IV at a cost of £6,000. It is far the most magnificent, and has an elaborate jewel-encrusted scabbard and hilt. Each of the other three swords has a symbolic meaning. They are plainer and have red velvet scabbards ornamented with gold braid. The oldest, historically, is the short pointless Sword of Mercy known as Curtana. It is first mentioned by name at the Coronation of Eleanor of Provence, the wife of Henry III, in 1236. The two other swords represent Spiritual Justice and Temporal Justice.

Something has been said in an earlier chapter of the symbolic significance of the Orb and the Sceptres which are placed in the Sovereign's hands immediately before the Crowning. The Orb was made in 1661. It is a golden globe six inches in diameter, surmounted by a great amethyst upon which is a jewelled cross. The Sceptre with the Cross or Royal Sceptre is about three feet long with a gem-encrusted handle. Above the stem was inserted in 1911 the largest portion of the Star of Africa diamond ($516\frac{1}{2}$ carats), and above this again is a superb amethyst on which rests a jewelled cross. During the actual Crowning another Sceptre, the Rod of Equity—also known as the Sceptre with the Dove—takes the place of the Orb in the Sovereign's left hand. It is about three and a half feet long, of gold, with jewelled bands and handle. The Sceptre is surmounted by a gold ball on which is a white enamelled dove with wings out-stretched. The eyes, beak, and feet are of gold. A sceptre with a dove, typifying the Holy Ghost, has been carried by English Kings since at least the 12th century.

The Crown of a Queen Consort is specially made for her Coronation. The Crown worn by Queen Elizabeth, the Queen Mother, contained the Koh-i-Noor diamond. There are also two Sceptres, resembling those of the Sovereign but slightly smaller. They were made for Queen Mary of Modena, the wife of King James II.

THE AMPULLA: THE SPOON

The Anointing of a Sovereign at a Coronation traces its origin to the Old Testament account of the anointing of Saul and David by Samuel. It was a jealously guarded privilege confined originally to the Kings of England, France, Jerusalem, and Sicily. France claimed that their Kings were anointed with oil which had been specially brought down from Heaven. A somewhat similar legend was current in England where the Oil was said to have been given to Thomas Becket, when in exile, by the Blessed Virgin. The Oil is now placed at a Coronation in the Golden Eagle or Ampulla (*left*) which is possibly part of the original Regalia and escaped destruction during the Cromwellian period. The Oil, when required, is poured through the beak of the Eagle into the Spoon (*below*) of which the handle is unquestionably of the 13th century.

The illustration at the top of the page is interesting as it is one of the highly fanciful Dutch engravings that were published after the Coronation of William III and Mary II. It is quite inaccurate but it purports to show the Anointing. The Archbishop of Canterbury appears to be anointing the King on the breast, at his side the Dean of Westminster holds a salver upon which is a flagon containing the Holy Oil. Another prelate holds William's vestments which have been removed, and at the same time the Queen is presented with the Bible. What Romyn de Hooghe, the artist, intended to convey by the actions of the two bishops behind the King is not known.

The Coronation Ring worn by King George VI. The centre stone is a sapphire, four narrow rubies represent the Cross of St George.

THE SYMBOL OF KINGLY POWER AND JUSTICE

The Sceptre with the Cross, the head of which is seen below (*right*), was made for Charles II. The Star of Africa Diamond at the top of the stem is so set that it can be removed and worn as a pendant. Above it is a remarkable amethyst mounted by jewelled fillets and surmounted by a jewelled *cross pattée*. The Sceptre with the Dove (*left*) has a white enamelled dove at its summit. A medieval King is shown holding an earlier form of sceptre headed by a cluster of leaves. Below, King George VI holds the Sceptre with the Cross in his right hand and the Sceptre with the Dove in his left.

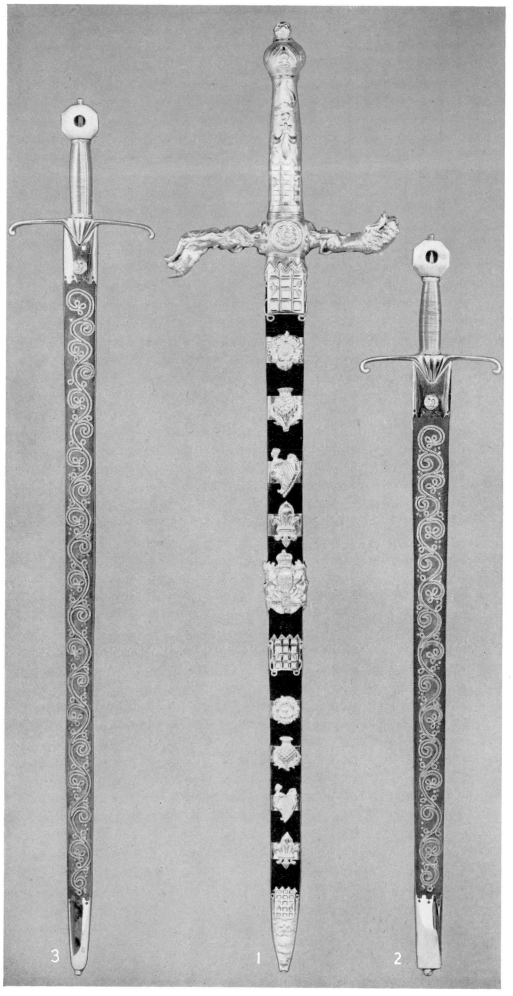

THE SWORDS

Each of the Swords carried before the Sovereign at a Coronation is symbolic of Royal Majesty. The two-handed Sword of State (1) is the emblem of authority; Curtana, or the unpointed sword (2), symbolises Royal Mercy; the two identical swords (3) represent respectively justice to the Spirituality and justice to the Temporality. The fourth, or Jewelled Sword, is the Sovereign's personal sword. This is the sword used at the girding (see page 31) during the Service which is personally offered at the Altar by the Sovereign and afterwards redeemed in a beautiful act of symbolism.

Three swords were carried before Richard I at his Coronation in 1189. Curtana is first mentioned by name at the Coronation of Queen Eleanor, wife of Henry III.

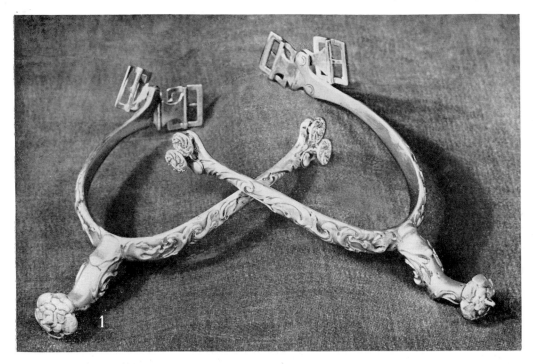

(1) The Spurs of solid gold with "pricks" and buckles were part of the Regalia made for the Coronation of Charles II. (2) St. Edward's Staff. This was also made in 1661. It is now carried in the Procession but not otherwise used. It retains its ancient name, and it is a curious fact that in the Bayeux Tapestry Edward the Confessor is represented holding a long pointed staff which closely resembles the present staff. (3) The Gold Chalice, engraved with the Royal Arms, which is used during the Coronation Service. (4) The Mace. This is one of the eight Maces of which the earliest was made for the Coronation of Charles II. They are of silver gilt, chased and ornamented with the emblems of the United Kingdom.

9

THE MUSIC

USIC has been a prominent feature of Coronations from the earliest times. Some of the anthems still sung at certain places in the Service have come down to us from the 10th century. Thus the anthem "Zadok the priest and Nathan the prophet anointed Solomon king" has been sung at the Anointing from, at least, the Coronation of King Edgar in 973. It may, however, be doubted whether the "many antemys i-song by note," which are mentioned as having been sung at the Coronation of Henry VI, can be classed as anthems in the modern sense of the word. Probably they were the psalms, or portions of psalms, already in the Service which were sung to their ordinary plain-song chants. It was not until the passing of plain-song from the ordinary church services at the Reformation that the opportunity came for the secular composers. Henceforth, although the words were the same, the settings to which they were sung became increasingly varied.

The result was, as might have been expected, that the influence of the organists of Westminster Abbey and of the Chapel Royal became predominant in the music sung at Coronations. They were in charge of the music, and it was but natural that they should compose the anthems and music required in the Service. Gibbons, Blow, Purcell, and Croft were all organists of Westminster Abbey; Tomkins, Child, Boyce, Turner, Henry Lawes, and Jeremiah Clarke were either organists or connected with the Chapel Royal; and these were the composers who provided practically all the music of 17th- and 18th-century Coronations. At the Coronation of George II in 1727 a notable exception was made when the greatest composer of the age, Handel, specially wrote for the occasion the four great anthems "The King shall rejoice," "Zadok the Priest," "My heart is inditing," and "Let thy hand be strengthened." Of these this setting of "Zadok" has retained its unquestioned place in the Service to the present day.

A further change came at the Coronation of George IV in 1821. The King was a genuine lover of music and took a personal interest in the music for his Coronation. It was by his command that the "Hallelujah" chorus was sung on his entry into the Abbey. It was also sung at Queen Victoria's Coronation after the *Gloria in Excelsis*. It was not, however, until a century later that any attempt was made to make the music representative of English music as a

93

ACKNOWLEDGMENTS

The author is indebted to Sir Vincent Baddeley for kindly allowing him to quote on page 78 the note made by Lord John Thynne in the copy of the Service Book used by him at the Coronation of Queen Victoria.

The publishers gratefully acknowledge the assistance rendered by the governing bodies of the following in tracing and identifying many illustrations of historic interest: Westminster Abbey Muniments Room; British Museum; Victoria and Albert Museum; Guildhall Museum, City of London; University Library, Cambridge; Westminster Public Library and Birmingham Reference Library. Facilities for photographing MSS., prints, and drawings were granted and in some cases negatives were made available.

The photographs of the Regalia are reproduced by authority of the Controller of Her Majesty's Stationery Office and are Crown Copyright. The copyright is reserved of the portrait of Queen Victoria on page 80.

For permission to use the photograph of the Royal Arms (facing the portrait of the Queen) the publishers are indebted to Wessex Film Productions Ltd., producers of *Royal Heritage*, the documentary film which portrays the true and vital meaning of the Coronation Ceremony. A book of the same title illustrated with photographs from the film is published by Pitkin Pictorials Ltd.

The half-tone engravings (with the exception of the frontispiece) were made by W. F. Sedgwick Ltd., photographic engravers to His late Majesty, King George V. It should be appreciated that a number of the plates had to be engraved from originals of considerable antiquity. Several of the photographs of the Coronation of King George VI were taken by means of tele-photo lens under poor lighting conditions and were therefore of indifferent quality.

BIBLIOGRAPHY

The following are among the principal works consulted:

The Letters of Queen Victoria, 1908. (John Murray.)

Crown and Empire, 1937. (The Times Publishing Co.)

Anon: *Chapters on Coronations*, 1838.

Jones, Wm.: *Crowns and Coronations*, 1898.

Macleane, D.: *The Great Solemnity of the Coronation*, 1911.

Novello, Messrs.: *The Music for the Coronations of Edward VII, George V and George VI*. (Published separately in 1902, 1911 and 1937.)

Ogilby, J.: *Entertainment of Charles II*, 1662.

Planché, J. R.: *Regal Records*, 1838.

Sandford, F.: *The History of the Coronation . . . King James II*, 1687.

Schramm, P. E.: *A History of the English Coronation*, 1937.

Stanley, A. P.: *Memorials of Westminster Abbey*. (5th ed. 1882.)

Taylor, A.: *The Glory of Regality*, 1820.

Wickham Legg, L. G.: *English Coronation Records*, 1901.

    „   „   „   *Three Coronation Orders*, 1900. (H. Bradshaw Society.)

Wordsworth, Chr.: *The Manner of the Coronation of King Charles I*, 1892. (H. Bradshaw Society.)

Younghusband, G., and C. Davenport: *The Crown Jewels of England*, 1919.

Westminster Abbey Muniments and British Museum MSS.

Articles in *The Ancestor* (Vols. 1 and 2); *The English Historical Review* (Vol. XXII); *The Nineteenth Century* (May 1937); *History* (March 1937); *The Times* (27th March, 1937 and 20th February, 1937); *Cornhill Magazine* (May 1937); *Speculum* (Vol. XIV), etc.

Contemporary accounts of Coronations in various Lives and Autobiographies—including *King George V His Life and Reign* by Harold Nicolson and *The Age of Elegance* by Arthur Bryant.

THE HISTORY OF THE CORONATION

RENCE E. TANNER, M.V.O., V.P.S.A